Interceding with Jesus

Bellwether

Mother Nadine

Intercessors of the Lamb
Omaha, NE

Published by the Intercessors of the Lamb

Additional copies of this book may be obtained through our web page store at or by contacting:

Intercessors of the Lamb
4014 North Post Road
Omaha, NE 68112
402-455-0188
e-mail: bellwether@novia.net
web page: www.bellwetheromaha.org

Library of Congress Catalog Card Number: 00-136377

ISBN: 0-9664956-1-6

Printed in the United States of America.

"Therefore, Jesus is always
able to save those
who approach God
through Him
since He lives forever
to make intercession for them"
(Heb 7:25).

Interceding with Jesus

An Introduction to Intercessory Prayer

Methods of Prayers

Opening Prayer

"Holy Spirit, we come to You because we know that without Your overshadowing and presence, we would be in the dark. So we ask for a special outpouring of Your presence upon us as we read this book. We ask for a new anointing every day of Your presence. We ask that we may be empty vessels filled only with Your light, Your truth, Your discernment, Your power. We ask that the Father may receive greater honor and glory. We ask that we may always be in union with Jesus, King of all hearts, and with Mary our Mother, Queen of all hearts. We implore you, dear Blessed Mother, to be our very special intercessor, to obtain for each one of us the graces, the lights, the gifts, the blessings that you know the Spirit wants to pour out upon us. In your care, we ask you Mary, to continue to teach us wisdom and to teach us love. We pray this as always in Jesus' name. Amen."

Forward

It's right next to the Roman Coliseum where many of our early brothers and sisters in the faith gave the ultimate testimony to Christ. Walk past the ancient ruins where the gladiators once lived and trained, and you come to St. Clement's Church where the third successor to St. Peter is buried. Enter and behold the mosaic in the apse of the Church and you will see why Christianity triumphed over paganism then and why it will triumph now.

This magnificent mosaic depicts the Cross as the Tree of Life, planted in the New Eden. From this glorious cross where God died that we might live comes forth the living waters of grace and an explosion of green vegetation filled with the animals and birds and Saints and cities of the New Creation, the Church. From the Sacrifice of Christ, from His pierced side, flows forth the grace and life and healing and holiness which we now enjoy. I put "flows" in the present tense not only because the mosaic still captures it but primarily because this Life-Giving Offering is going on now for us and for the whole world as the Victim Lamb lives to make intercession for us.

Mother Nadine has put this mosaic into words and shaped it into a whole lifestyle in this book, *Interceding with Jesus*. At the center of the world and at the center of the intercessor's life is the life-giving cross of Jesus. The Risen Lamb is looking for intercessors who will embody His on-going self-offering and intercession before the Father on behalf of sinners. The conditions are deep contemplative union with Jesus and a willingness to share His crucified love for this world.

Just as the church of St. Clements is built on previous churches in his honor going all the way back to the first Christian century, so Mother Nadine's teaching and charism is built on many holy men and women who went before her. One can sense in this book the smiling presence of St. Therese of the Child Jesus whose childlike trust in the Heavenly Father was tested by deep trials of faith and blossomed into a blazing zeal and fruitful intercession for the Church's missions. From St. John Eudes, the first founder of the Good Shepherd Sisters, this spiritual daughter draws such treasures as the beautiful union of the two Hearts of Jesus and Mary and the conviction that Jesus wants to live his life again in every Christian, including His office of Calvary intercession. Finally, one hears in these pages echoes of the teaching and personality of St. Teresa of Avila— the call to contemplation and transforming union and the cross, the endearing qualities of a warm humanity, good common sense and a boundless sense of humor and good cheer.

Finally, the reader will want to keep this book close at hand. It is both an inspiration and a practical guide. The author's stories, personal experiences and choice of Scriptural quotes weave together a rich contemplative spirituality which will continue to inspire and challenge us. How good it is to know that intercession is basically wanting what God already wants for people and asking Him to do it. And how refreshing it is to be taught the simple methods of prayer that God has given to Mother Nadine and the Intercessors of the Lamb. She teaches us how even a child can "intercede with Jesus."

Fr. Richard Tomasek, S.J.
Director of Spiritual Formation
Pontifical College Josephinum
Columbus, Ohio

You are Sacrament

You are a sign of the gentleness of God.
> You are a symbol of the smile of Divinity.
Intercessor of the Lamb, do you know your sacramental power?
> The transforming power of the Church is yours
>> carried in the delicate vessel of your word,
>> your prayer, your heart.
> You are sacrament!
You smile and through your eyes must radiate the Son of God.
For you are sacrament.
> You warmly clasp a hand
>> and the wheat-grains of a heart are changed to Christ.

For you are sacrament.
You endure with spirit-filled courage the wood of the Cross,
> which is warmed by the Body of Christ.
For indeed you are sacrament.
You must love and in your love the world will encounter God.
> Intercessor, what price the emptying of the vessel
>> that you may serve as instrument, as sacramental channel.
It is the price of parenthood,
Of bringing forth life in the Spirit and in the Body.
Being willing to die to your own desires,
> to sacrifice, to be vulnerable
It is the price of parenthood, nurturing development
> in patience, pain and prayer.

It is the price of giving birth.
> Your life consumed upon a paten
>> that the life of Christ may be chaliced.
Is the price too high, O Intercessor who is sacrament?
> Is it too high?
Do you not know that love knows no counting.
> That fire does not measure as it consumes.
If in being sacrament I house the God I channel,
> then bless the water of my openness, touch my earthen
> shell, ordain me, God, with the oil of joy!
>> Amen.

Chapter 1

"Lord, Teach Us to Pray"
Lk 11:1

One day we received a phone call from a teacher inquiring the whereabouts of a young boy who had somehow given our phone number as his emergency phone number at school. Maybe he didn't think that there was such a phone number, but now this school teacher was calling asking us about the whereabouts of a young boy whom we didn't even know! Obviously, this boy was playing hooky, and so we started to pray for him and as we prayed, we were strongly led to pray for all runaways. We prayed for this boy and for all runaways for several days, and that was it.

Later that week, we received a phone call from New York. The caller said that a young teenage girl had run away from home and her parents were absolutely frantic wondering where she was. We could just imagine the terrible way the parents must be feeling and we were terrified at all the things that could possibly be happening to this girl. When we first got this prayer burden to pray for all runaways, she had been missing for a week already, but on that very day that we began to pray for all runaways, she called her parents from California and told them where she was!

Lord, teach us to pray!

Many years ago, a woman would come to us and ask for prayer that she could stop smoking. I think everybody in Omaha had prayed for this woman to stop smoking, but she kept smoking and smoking, and yet she was always asking for prayer. Priests would pray, special prayer teams would pray, but she still kept smoking. She couldn't break the habit. One night we were at a prayer meeting and a young man whom we had never seen before was there and he just kind of glowed with the presence of God. Everybody noticed. He was just passing through. Who knows—maybe he was an angel! After the prayer meeting was over, everyone made a beeline to this young man for prayer because there was something special about him.

I was standing in line for prayer and right in front of me was this woman who wanted to stop smoking. I thought, "Oh, I know what she's going to ask for. We've heard it for a year." I couldn't help but overhear because I was the next one in line and when it was her turn, he said, "What would you like prayer for?" She said, "To stop smoking." He paused for a moment and I realized he was checking something out with the Lord. Then he said to her, "Do you **want** to stop smoking?" I kind of muttered to the Lord silently, "Of course she wants to stop smoking. She's been asking all of us for a year to stop smoking." Well the young man waited for her reply and there was this silence. I thought, "Isn't this strange? She's not answering him." We waited some more and then I could see the struggle going on within her. Finally she said, "No, I really don't want to stop. I should quit for health reasons, but I really don't want to stop." So then he said, "Let's pray for the desire for you to want to stop."

The prayer that needed to be prayed was "Lord, please give her the desire to quit." So this young man prayed that she would get that desire to quit smoking and the desire for her will to be one with God's desire, and that she would be able to quit smoking without any problem.

Lord, teach us to pray.

A few years ago, one of the Sisters and I were on our way to South Bend, Indiana, and we got off the interstate at the wrong exit and got caught in all that awful traffic outside of Chicago. It's six lanes, bumper to bumper; it must have been rush hour. We were delayed and we could have gotten all fidgety about it, "Oh my goodness, we're going to be late. Why didn't we listen and take the right route?" We could have gone on and on grumbling with all these inner conversations but right away we thought, "There has to be a reason this happened. Nothing happens by chance." *Nothing* when we're moving with the Lord.

So we started watching, "There's something on this interstate that You want us to pray for and we're going to watch for it." We hadn't been stuck on the interstate for more than ten minutes when we saw this car clear over in the left lane start to inch its way over to try to get to the off ramp. By the time the car got to us, we just sat there and made room for it to get in front of us. The driver turned and looked at us and that was it! He saw we were nuns and the communication was tremendous! His look was, "I'm desperate, help me." I thought, "Lord, he's ready to take his own life." Both of us knew it. Here was the reason we had missed the turn—someone needed hope, someone needed grace, someone needed God, and there we were! God put him right in front of us. This man couldn't get to the ramp without passing right in front of us. I'll never forget that and we prayed, "Lord, please give this man all the graces he needs right now. Fill him with Your love and hope. Help him to want to live."

Lord, teach us to pray.

These stories illustrate what intercessory prayer is really about. True intercessory prayer is **prayer to the Father, through Jesus, led and empowered by the Holy Spirit.** Too often what we think of as intercessory prayer is really a prayer of petition. It's me telling God what I'd like Him to do, but when we are in intercession, we are being led and directed by the Holy Spirit on what to pray about and how to pray. In each of these situations, we were not the ones initiating the prayer. It was always God getting our attention, and once He pointed out a situation, we responded by asking God to do something about it. If we had used our natural sense, we would have completely missed the prayer that needed to be prayed, but when the Holy Spirit is the guide and leader in our prayer, we will see lives being touched and changed. Wherever we are, we need to be open and readily available to be used by the Holy Spirit.

Karl Rahner was a wonderful German theologian who wrote a great deal on the Church and the Sacraments. One of the things he said that most impressed me was that the Christian of the future must be a mystic or he or she will not persevere. That's pretty strong, isn't it? We must be mystics, all of us, but just what is a mystic? A mystic is someone who is connecting with God. Mystics are usually the little ones, the weak ones, the children. St. John talks about that, "As for you, the anointing you received from him remains in your hearts. This means you have no need for anyone to teach you. Rather, as his anointing teaches you about all things and is true—free from any lie—

remain in him as that anointing taught you" (1Jn 2:27). We need to be hearing from the Lord every day. We are the ones who are standing in need of God.

This reminds me of the song, "It's *me*, it's me O Lord, standing in the need of prayer. Not my brother, not my sister but it's me, O Lord, standing in the need of prayer." In our prayer, everything is gift and we just receive, and receive, and receive. We might receive love. We might receive the presence of God Himself. When Elizabeth of the Trinity would go into prayer, she would say, "I just sink into my Three." She could get there quickly. She could get all the distractions out and she could get into the silence of that inner communication with the Trinity, into that Divine cycle of Love, into that Family. We can get there, too, because of Jesus. He has opened the way. He has opened the door right into that Heart, into that Family. We're family now.

Children are wonderful intercessors. They have that basic humility that they know that without God they can do nothing. One of my favorite experiences of this was when I saw this tiny little girl, about three years old, named Angel. She was raised in a very Charismatic family lifestyle, and often saw her parents and grandparents lay their hands on people for healing. They were visiting some friends in Florida and her little playmate, Roger, fell down and got this big bump on his forehead. Angel asked her grandmother, "Would you please pray over Roger, he's hurt!" The grandmother said very wisely, "Angel, you know how to pray. God answers your prayers, too. You pray over Roger." So she went over and put her little hands on this big bump and she said, "Jesus, please heal Roger," and the bump shrank and disappeared just like that!

We all learned something that day—"with a little child to guide them" (Is 11:6). Here was our model intercessor—a child. We have a priest on our Board, and he has always said, "If I ever get sick, call in the children! They know how to get to God's heart, and He answers them." This shows us the beautiful fruit of the relationship with the Father. We know we are children, that's why we call Him "Abba," Daddy. That's how we relate to Him—as Father and child. We know our weaknesses, we know our littleness, and we know that our Daddy can do anything. He's big, He's powerful, He's loving, He's kind, He's good.

God is good, and He is good to us! We need the relationship with Jesus, Who is the Intercessor par excellence. The Father always hears Jesus.

So we need to become mystics—we need to hear God. It's essential for intercessors. We have to know who it is that's enlightening us. God's light is far greater than our natural light, so we are drawn to the Light Himself. The gift of reading hearts only comes from God. Even the Cure d'Ars couldn't read what was in the hearts of those he counseled unless God informed him. Intercessors can read hearts at times but it is only because it is God showing us, "I want to touch this heart. This is how I want to do it." Many people will come asking for prayer. They may be saying they need prayer for one thing but instead we may be picking up on another area that needs prayer even more. Maybe we sense their hopelessness or we can see and feel their loneliness. The heart has it's own language, and it knows. It's an intuitive gift that the Spirit activates in teaching us how to pray. The beautiful thing about intercessors is that their main gift is that they *simply ask the Lord to do what He has already revealed that He wants to do.*

God stands behind that intercessor, but for an intercessor to know what to do and how to ask, many of the other gifts of the Spirit need to be working. Intercessors have a gift of knowledge, not that prophetic "thus says the Lord" knowledge, but they know God's mind and His heart because through their relationship with the Father they understand; they know what He wants. At times, intercessors may have the gift of healing, but it's not really the full-fledged gift of healing. It's a gift of intercession working through the gift of healing. God is just saying, "I want this person healed, just ask Me to do it. I'll use you as My instrument."

At times intercessors may be able to read a heart, but that doesn't mean they have the gift of reading hearts. If God wants you to know what's going on in a heart on a particular day, He will tell you. Perhaps someone is going to commit suicide, so He will give you the direction on how to pray to prevent it. We're just totally available and open to pray the prayer that God wants us to pray; we just ask Him to do what He has already revealed to us that He wants to do, and He does. This is the gift of intercession.

Intercession incorporates all the gifts of the Holy Spirit. A priest used to call me every Saturday night to intercede for his sermons on Sunday. He would call and ask me to pray and I would say, "Ask the Lord. He'll be there. Ask God." So to preach, teach, or to do any ministry well, we have to ask for God's power and His grace so that hearts will be touched.

All ministries hook into the ministry of intercession. Imagine a huge umbrella representing the Church. It has many different spokes, with each spoke representing the different ministries of the Church, but the pole of the umbrella, the stem of the umbrella is intercession. As the pole stabilizes the spokes of the umbrella and enables them to do their job, so too intercessors stabilize the Church and enable it to do its job in a special way. Intercessors stabilize ministries because it is out of this deep prayer of intercession that God's graces and His powers will flow to all ministries. As the focus of the umbrella is never on the pole but on the beautiful canopy of color, most people will not even be aware of the intercession that has gone on. All the time spent in intercessory prayer may even seem like a waste of time to some people who are busy "doing," but it is through this union in intercessory prayer that God will show us how to pray according to His heart's desire, and then He will shower down His graces and power upon His people.

I had a dear friend who is no longer living, but he called me one day in tears. He was listening to the six o'clock news and a little baby was going to die because there wasn't an available heart transplant for this baby. They waited and waited and no heart. A heart transplant had to be right in all the chemistry and everything, and so their last chance now was to send the baby out to Los Angeles to a top hospital and wait for a heart. The baby wouldn't live more than 24 hours if a heart didn't come through. Now here's my friend who had just heard this on the news, bursting into tears. He never had any children of his own, and his heart was so filled with compassion that he was sobbing that this baby had to have a heart. So right then, I said, "You're the intercessor—you have the burden placed on your heart. That's the Lord. This is His compassion. God has given you His feelings of love for the child. God wants *you* to ask Him to send the baby a heart." So he prayed and the baby got a heart the next day! Isn't that beautiful?!

Lord, teach us to pray.

Trust the leading of your heart. Trust your feelings especially when you're so filled with love for a person or a situation, because that love is God's love and He is putting it into your heart. It is God's compassion and love that heals. God is Love. There's no doubt about it.

In intercessory prayer, we don't know the outcome of our prayer and this will keep us humble of heart. We don't always know for sure and we can never become dogmatic thinking, "I know that this is what God wants." The words we use are, "*I sense* that this might be the leading of the Lord." If I'm honest about it and I truthfully am sensing that this is what God wants, God will honor that and won't let me hurt myself or anybody else. He will show you.

So if you believe the Lord is prompting you to pray in a particular way, go ahead and pray. If it doesn't bear fruit, then it can be a learning lesson for you, too. Our attitude is so important. We don't want to ever get to the point of, "The Lord said this and that is it." We never can be that sure that we know God's mind. We must be commissioned in prayer, so it is key that we wait for the green light from the Lord.

The Apostles were commissioned by Jesus, "Go, therefore, and make disciples of all the nations" (Mt 28:19). We must be given the "go ahead" by the Commander and Chief. So sometimes we will get strong signals on how to pray and sometimes we will get mixed signals. Sometimes we will get little weak signals, but that is God, always giving us a signal, communicating to us to bring the situation back to Him, so we can ask for His guidance. He wants to move. He wants to tell us more. He has the time. He has the energy. He has the power. He has the vision. He has everything He needs to help anybody in any situation. Miracles are easy for God. He loves us so much!

Lord, teach us to pray!

Chapter 2

The Lifestyle of an Intercessor
"It's the life that prays"

We are going to focus on the intercessor and who he is because **it is the life that prays.** It's who we are that really prays. It's the intercessor and his relationship with the Father, Son, and Holy Spirit that are the key to intercession but there are things we can do and things we can avoid doing to enhance this relationship. We want our being, our very self, and who we are becoming to be so intertwined with the essence of who Jesus is that the Father cannot distinguish between the two of us.

Loves much

First of all, an intercessor is someone who **loves.** St. Teresa of Avila said that one who loves much prays much. Intercessors pray because their hearts are so filled with love that they can't help but pray! When one loves with the intensity of real love, then he really doesn't need to be taught how to do it. We don't need to be taught how to love because it's something that comes from deep within; it just wells up and overflows! This is true also with prayer: it comes from deep within, wells up, and overflows from our heart. "The water I give shall become a fountain within him, leaping up to provide eternal life" (Jn 4:14).

As there are so many different ways to express love, there are also numerous ways to express that love in our prayer. Prayer will always be new and exciting! As we can always find new, creative ways to love, we can likewise always find new ways to pray.

In the cloister, we were professional pray-ers but, believe it or not, I was living with women who were professional lovers.

They knew how to love. That's all we were taught: how to love the Father, how to love Jesus, and how to love the Spirit. Then we were taught how to allow the Father, Son and Holy Spirit to love us. It was from receiving the love of the Trinity that our hearts grew and we were able to carry people and their concerns deep within our hearts.

An intercessor loves much. We are filled with God's love and this is why we want to give. We want to do things for others. We want others to experience God's love. God's greatest joy is to give to us. "God so loved the world that he gave his only Son, that whoever believes in him may not die but may have eternal life" (Jn 3:16).

An intercessor daily prays for the ability to love as Jesus loved. If this ability to love deeply is not a desire deep within his heart, he prays for this desire. We must understand that the ability to hold all these people and concerns of God within our heart is a gift from the Father, pure gift. We must never take it for granted and must pray often for this gift to be used within us.

Union with God

God is initiating this call to union with Him. **He** is calling us. It is God who initiates prayer. God, being the Lover, initiates everything. He has given us the call to be intercessors. We do not take it on by ourselves. We are called. He is calling us to the ministry of intercession. Prayer **is** the intercessor. It's not that you will catch intercessors in prayer between five and six PM, but rather it's a prayer of the heart that takes over every waking moment. Becoming the prayer is the way of life for the intercessor; it's the life that prays.

We are precious to God. He wants to hear us and answer our prayers. God, refers to us as His beloved, and says to the soul, "Arise, my beloved, my beautiful one, and come! . . . let me hear your voice" (Sng 2:10-14). That's the beauty of contemplative prayer! That's the beauty of love and this love union with God. He wants to hear *us*, He wants us to speak to Him. Sometimes we may speak to Him because of our personal needs, but other times when we are in the power of intercession, we go before Him because of love. The love for the people we're praying for wells up within us and draws us to the Father, pleading on their behalf. There is a power in this depth of love and God honors that in a special way.

As the Apostles "devoted themselves to constant prayer" (Acts 1:14), the intercessor also commits his whole life to **union with God**. Prayer is really nothing more than an instrument, like the telephone, to communicate with God. If you keep the image of a phone in your mind you won't get too hung up on a particular prayer form or that you have to pray in a certain way. When we're talking on the phone, we are hardly conscious of the instrument we're using; it's just the voice at the other end that we focus on. It's the same with prayer—our focus is on the voice at the other end. Prayer is simply connecting with the Father, Son, and Holy Spirit. We use our prayer to connect, and once we've connected, we aren't even conscious of how we got there. We are receiving God's Word, Jesus.

The Holy Spirit will take us into the desert to experience that deep inner presence of God Himself. "The woman was given the wings of a gigantic eagle so that she could fly off to her place in the desert" (Rv 12:14). As intercessors, we are also called to allow these eagle wings, which are contemplative spirituality and prayer, to carry us off to a place in the desert every day. When we come to that desert, we're being brought to **silence**, which is so essential within the intercessor's life. Jesus knew how necessary it was for us to come into that inner silence, into that listening mode so that we could hear Him. He said, "Whenever you pray, go to your room, close your door, and pray to your Father in private" (Mt 6:6). Shut out the other thoughts, shut out all the things we have to do or the things we haven't done. Shut it all out. Get into that inner solitude and pray to the Father in secret. It's in that inner solitude, in that inner silence, in that inner desert, in that Promised Land within all of us—this is where God lives.

I love the Scripture where it says that there is a special place that has been prepared for us by God. Jesus said, "I am indeed going to prepare a place for you" (Jn 14:3). God thinks we're special and He has prepared a place for us as St. John tells us. He wants us to be alone with Him. He wants us to be loved by Him. He wants us to be taught by Him. This is absolutely key for anyone called to the ministry of intercession. This intimacy, this special place of prayer, this special place of aloneness, this desert that's deep within us, needs to be nurtured by God every day.

God tells us, "I will allure her (lure her, lure the Church, lure each individual soul); I will lead her into the desert and speak to her heart" (Hos 2:16). God is the lover; we are the beloved and it is so important for us to go to this place of aloneness with God to allow ourselves to be lured to the desert where He can speak to us. If we don't have a thirst or a desire for this intimacy, all we have to do is to ask for this gift. He will give us a thirst for Him. He will give us a hunger for Him. He will create some kind of desire in our hearts just for Him. We need a time of intimacy, a time of infilling for ourselves before we pray for others. When we are finished being filled up, the people of God will still be there needing us but there has to be a feeding time for an intercessor first.

We have to take our cars to the filling station for gas every now and then or they're not going to run. We can't run on empty, either. Much of the burnout in the Church today is not because people are engaged in too much ministry; it's because people are not receiving enough of God's love and nurturing. God's words are words of spirit and life, "The words I spoke to you are spirit and life" (Jn 6:63). It is essential that we receive this life, that we get filled up, and remain in this deep level of union at all times. It is God's love that will bring forth healing. We can only give out of the abundance of our hearts. We cannot give something we ourselves do not have, so we have to receive the Lord and His love in its fullness each day. God may stretch us from day to day so that the fullness of Him within us will increase, but for today maybe I only have a thimble space for Him to enter in. He'll fill it. Maybe tomorrow I might have room for a whole barrel. My heart just might have expanded and He'll fill it. God always wants to fill us. He's always wanting to give. God is love and the nature of love is to give.

Jesus tells us, "I know my sheep and my sheep know me" (Jn 10:14). When God uses the word "know" it means "experience." My sheep *experience* Me. There really isn't any other way to know God except through experiencing Him. While speaking at a conference in California, we had some delicious orange juice for breakfast. It was orange-orange! We don't experience that in Nebraska, but let's take orange juice for

17

example. An expert can tell me where oranges are grown, what is the best climate for the trees, when the trees should be planted, and when the fruit is ready to be picked. A nutritionist can come along and tell me all the reasons why I should drink orange juice and the wonderful things it's going to do for me. I can study an orange and learn all about it, but I can't really tell you what an orange is until I taste it. I have to experience it. It has to be my own experience. I have to taste it myself.

It's the same with intercessory prayer. We can study about God, and it is important to learn as much as we can about God, especially through Scripture, but we have to touch Him. We have to taste God. We have to experience Him to know Him. Then once we know Him, we will know how to pray. This is what John the contemplative knew. He knew Jesus' heart so well, and this is our goal: to come to know God's mind and heart. When we pray, we come into a listening posture where we can hear the Lord. This listening posture is extremely important as the foundation of all our prayer, and once we hear from the Lord, then we pray the prayer that is on God's mind and heart, the prayer He has revealed to us in prayer.

Believing Intercession

I believe God is seeking intercessors today to ask that our entire Church and our entire nation be spared. It doesn't take many people praying, a remnant is sufficient, but what it does take is **believing intercession**. We have to believe that God cares. It can require all of our trust and belief in God because we're most vulnerable when we're in this level of intercession. So when we speak of "believing intercession" what we're talking about is this faith walk. It's believing that God *can* help us, that God *wants* to help us, and that He *will* help us even when the outlook is terribly bleak. It's believing that God has our own concerns foremost in His heart, so that we can trust God and forget about our needs and concerns, leaving us free to focus on praying for others.

St. Martin, Bishop of Tours, is a beautiful example of believing intercession. There is a story that is told about him. His country was in a mess just like ours but rather than giving up in despair, he was gazing at it through those spiritual eyes in prayer. There were so many problems that he didn't even know where to begin to pray, but he believed that the Lord cared and that He would answer his prayer. He went into prayer one time really grieving, "O Lord, what would it take to spare my country? What would it take?" The Lord said, "Martin, it will take one saint." Isn't that hopeful? "One saint." That's the power of holiness. If God could find ten, fifty, or even one hundred saints in America, imagine how He could move!

Prayer is always for others

Intercessors also have specific needs that God will meet. He will meet the needs of intercessors. We can count on Him to take care of us so our **prayer is always for others.** This is why it's such a powerful prayer. It's not directed towards self at all. It falls into the realm of charity and God being Love, loves anything we do in that line of charity. Our prayer is for others.

When Fr. DiOrio first came to Omaha he stayed with us for two weeks and one night he directed a wonderful session on intercessory prayer itself. People flocked to Fr. DiOrio for healing and they all came with a lot of serious concerns. For many people it was a matter of life and death; they needed miracles, so they were counting on that prayer ministry to bring forth miracles in their lives.

So here they come, and Fr. DiOrio says, first of all, "You may not pray for any personal concerns you have brought here tonight. You may only pray for others, your neighbor, the person sitting next to you, somebody else's burden, somebody else's sickness or illness, and that's it." You could hear a gasp throughout the whole church because that wasn't what they expected. They came to pray for their own healing, not someone else's. It was awesome! I can't tell you the healings that took place that night when these people did that! God healed them! People were healed of terminal cancer and blindness, people got up out of wheelchairs and walked, all because they had let go of their own self-interests, trusted in God to take care of them, and reached out and prayed for their neighbor. Tremendous blessings poured forth from their self-less love!

When I entered the cloister, one of the things the Lord told me from the very beginning was that I was not to pray for my family. Here I am in a cloister where all we do is pray and I'm not to pray for my own family! He said, "Your interest now is to be for My family. I'll have other people pray for your family." So I let them go and the fruit it has born in the lives of my nephews and family has been wonderful! Whoever their intercessors are, I'll certainly thank them someday. They are doing a much better job than I probably would be doing, and to this day, I'm still not the intercessor for my own family at all.

That doesn't mean to say you don't pray for your families. It means you have to listen to what God is saying. You have to listen to who God wants you to pray for, and sometimes it's not for those closest to you. He might want us to pray for those who don't like us or maybe for those we're having a hard time getting along with. We don't know until God shows us and puts it in our heart. So, intercessory prayer is always **prayer for others**. It's always prayer for others and this is why it has a power to it. Intercession is unselfish.

For the greater honor and glory of God

This is also one of the reasons why a lot of people are not in intercessory prayer ministry simply because "there's nothing in it for me." It's for somebody else and it is all **for the greater honor and glory of God**. I actually had a man tell me once, "I'm not interested in intercession because there's no glory in it for me. I pray, I suffer, I sacrifice, and somebody gets a grace, and I don't even get a thank you. They don't even know I'm alive." That's true, because intercessors are very hidden, but God knows who you are and He will reward you.

Being a convert to the Catholic faith, I have no idea of the cost of my conversion through someone else's prayers and sacrifices. I'll meet that person in Heaven someday. I have no idea who that person is or the price that was paid, but somebody heard God and prayed for me and I received tremendous graces to come into the Catholic faith. We never know who has prayed for many of the good things that happen in our lives, and we will never know many of the good things that have happened to a lot of people because we've prayed for them.

The focus of our prayer has to be on the Lord and His honor and glory. Intercessory prayer is a thankless type of prayer because rarely does anyone know you were in intercession for that person. There are times in God's plan when there is only one person in intercession for someone or something, and there are times when there are many intercessors in intercession for the same person or thing. God is the One who directs the prayer. So when we pray, we come into a listening posture, into the realm of intimacy where we can hear the Lord. This is extremely important as the foundation of all our prayer. Once we hear from the Lord, we must believe that He will do what He says.

Empty of self; full of God's love

I don't know of anyone that is more poor, in the good sense, than an intercessor. An intercessor, when he is really formed by the Spirit, by the Sanctifier, becomes very **empty of himself**. There is very little self involved in his prayer. St. John of the Cross talks about a poverty which leads to sanctity: "nada, nada, nada," meaning "nothing, nothing, nothing." This is the summit of sanctity when everything is totally given over for God (*The Ascent of Mount Carmel,* I,14,11). Our whole focus is on God and His ministry, His wishes, and His vision. So if we enter into that poverty of spirit where we don't have our own will or own spirit trying to get in God's way, then He hears us. He sees us as empty and poor. Mary was empty. In her Magnificat she said, "The hungry he has given every good thing" (Lk 1:53). If we come to prayer empty of ourselves, we'll go away filled and satisfied.

Intercessors are people full of God's love, full of God's power, obedient to the slightest movement of whatever He wants. That's all He's looking for. Jesus said, "Blest are they who hunger and thirst for holiness; they shall have their fill" (Mt 5:6). This is the deepest desire of an intercessor—to become a saint. St. Claude de la Columbiere used to pray everyday, "Oh Lord, make me a saint in spite of myself." We, too, should pray, "Make me a saint, Lord, in spite of myself!"

As a convert, I had a lot of different thoughts of what a saint was because I would read all these extreme things that the saints did, and I would try to imitate them. So if it meant sleeping on coat hangers for awhile, that's what I did. I read that the Cure d'Ars ate boiled potatoes every day, so that's what I did. Another saint wore a hair shirt, so I wore a hair shirt. I did everything I could to become a saint, but their sometimes extreme methods to achieve sanctity didn't seem to work out for me. Then I read the Scripture and thought, "Oh, to be a saint I just have to be full of *God's* love" (see Eph 1:4). Not self love, but full of God's love. Then I understood that to be a saint it takes a little dying every day to myself and my needs and desires. This is what God is asking of us. We have to kind of make room within our heart every day for God's love to fill us because there is a lot of self love in all of us. Once the Lord told me, "One of us has to go," and He said, "It's not going to be Me."

As we get rid of more and more of the selfish love within our hearts, then God's love can fill us and take over. As we surrender and open ourselves to receive this love, then we can spend all day long giving it away. Now we really have something to give to the world and to people—some of God's love. If we don't have a desire to become a saint, if we don't have a desire for intimacy with the Lord, then we won't understand why we should pray, and it's not our prayer that's the problem. The problem is that we need that hunger and thirst for holiness. When we read the lives of the saints, it was always this desire for union with God deep within their hearts that led their lives. It was absolutely key. So we may first have to check within our hearts to see if what we desire to become is what God desires us to become. We can have desires in our hearts that are not of God. They're our own desires but we have to let go of them and let the Lord plant His seeds in the vineyards of our hearts again.

Today it's very common to just accept and allow people and things to be as they are. Everyone's doing their own thing. There are many gray areas that we accept for the sake of compromise. But Jesus said, "He who is not with me is against me" (Mt 12:30). There isn't any middle ground. There isn't any gray area. There isn't any compromise. As intercessors we have to be careful of that. We must know ourselves, and we have to check our motives not only for what we do, but why we do something. We must always make sure we are operating in Jesus' Kingdom.

Approaches God with reverence

When we are in the presence of someone that we consider greater and more knowledgeable than ourselves, we become very silent and we listen. We are full of reverence and respect. Whenever the Holy Father walks into a crowded room, there probably isn't a peep out of anyone. We would be all ears to hear every word he said. That's the way it is when we come into the presence of God in prayer: holy awe. An intercessor always **approaches God with reverence**. Jesus "was heard because of his reverence" (Heb 5:7). Our attitude is to be full of holy awe. Many of the saints and prophets were heard because of their reverence, which came from their humility. They were willing to accept that child-like posture, that weak little lamb posture: "Without You, Lord, we cannot do anything. Without You we don't even know anything."

We do know that God hears us, and He wants to respond to us. That's why we're here. He needs us. Our country and our world needs us as well. So God encourages us, "When you call me," He's speaking directly to us, "when you go to pray to me, I will listen to you" (Jer 29:12). It is essential that we really believe that God cares, otherwise we would just be mouthing prayers, reciting petitionary types of prayer, and just speaking into the air. Jesus said, "In your prayer, do not rattle on like the pagans. They think they will win a hearing by the shear multiplication of words" (Mt 6:7). Our Lady at Medjugorje keeps reminding us that God doesn't need the multiplication of our words. He only wants that prayer of the heart. He wants our attitude of love, reverence, and compassion.

Identifies with others

Intercessors **identify** with the plight of those we pray for. We, too, have dark areas of sin in our lives no matter how hard we strive to avoid it. Sin is part of our fallen nature, so when we pray we don't say, "Please help those sinners over there. Please bless *them*." Rather we pray, "Lord, have mercy on *us*. *We* have fallen away from you. Please forgive *us*." This is how Moses prayed. He identified with his people. He had revelations from God and he would be up there on that mountaintop begging God to please spare His people. "Let your blazing wrath die down; relent in punishing your people. . . If you would only forgive their sin! If you will not, then strike me out of the book that you have written" (Ex 12:12, 32).

Like Moses, we are up there on that mountaintop anytime we're in prayer and we identify with whatever or whomever the Lord is asking us to pray for. If it's about our nation, its not all those sinners out there. It's me. Have mercy on *us*. I'm part of this human race. I'm part of this nation, of the sin of this nation, of the sin of the Church. Intercessors identify with whatever it is that God is saying to them. God can, and does, change His mind.

I had always heard that "Jesus Christ is the same yesterday, today, and forever" (Heb 13:8) and He is. God is Love. God can never be anything but Love. Intercessory prayer can, believe it or not, change the mind and heart of God. That's the power of intercession. Mary is asking for this in all of her major apparitions. She has said that through prayer we even have the power to stop war. This is true once we understand what God wants us to pray about and how He wants us to pray. When we really love and identify deeply with someone or something, whether it be with other people, our nation, or our Church, these are love burdens from God. He has placed His deep level of love and concern within us. He recognizes that we're coming to Him from deep within our hearts, and we know that He will listen because it's His love burden to begin with. God always hears the cry of the poor, always.

Respects other's privacy and secrecy

Intercessors can hold a lot of confidential information about the people, nations, governments, countries, Church officials, that God wants them to pray for. It can be anything. One of the principles for an intercessor is **respecting privacy and secrecy**. We don't tell. The information is for us so that we can come back and ask God to move, not to give us new gossip material. "Lord, this is what I'm understanding that You want me to ask You to do in this situation. Please do it." My prayer is very private between myself and the Lord. As God begins to trust us more with this kind of information, our intercession gets more powerful because as He's building a trust relationship with us, He is entrusting a tremendous amount of confidential information to us and we strive to become worthy of that trust.

When I came home from the cloister, I learned a great deal about this by being around doctor's wives. They have this kind of secrecy, too. They absolutely do not repeat what they hear. Never. And that's the way it is with an intercessor. Much of what we learn from God is just so we can tell God about situations and then ask Him to do it and that's it. It goes no further. We're not prophets that we have to go out and tell the world and tell others, "This is what's going to happen." No, when the Lord reveals what's going to happen to an intercessor, He reveals it so that the intercessor can come and say, "Lord, don't let that happen. Stop it, please." We don't just get information, panic, and say, "Oh my goodness. This is what the Lord's saying, and if we don't do this and this and this, then this is what's going to happen." Intercessors are people of tremendous hope because they're holding information and they know that God is saying, "Ask Me. I don't want this to happen. This is why I'm telling you what's in My mind and My heart. I don't want to do it. I want you now to ask Me not to do it."

Even when people call us for prayer and they spell out what they want us to pray for, we always ask the Lord first how we are to pray. Always. Maybe what they are asking for is what He wants to do but maybe it's not. We don't waste time praying about things people want, we only pray about what God wants. Many times what we want is what God wants, too, and He's put that desire in our hearts but we always check it out first. There are many times when we're praying for people and we have no idea who they are or what the total situation is, but God will take care of it.

You might wonder, "Is all this extra prayer really necessary? Shouldn't we spend our time and effort on doing something about all the problems in the world instead of working on becoming poor in spirit?" Social justice is quite "in" and there are many wonderful programs, but nothing's really going to happen in any of the programs, in any of the different avenues in the Church, without intercessors first asking God for the grace to give to these people out there in the different ministries. It's not that we shouldn't be active in the different ministries, but first of all, we need people praying for the graces to come. When Moses was in that powerful intercession on the mountaintop, the Amalekites had attacked the people of Israel and the Israelites were winning as long as Moses remained in intercession (Ex 17). We're not exactly winning out here in the Church today. We're certainly not winning many battles in America, but maybe it's because we're not there on the mountaintop enough, asking God to send the graces that people need. Maybe we're not begging for the graces of wisdom, knowledge, and understanding of His will and what He wants to do. We need His power, His presence through a new sovereign movement of the Holy Spirit to come and renew us and teach us truly how to pray.

Allowing the Father to pace us

One of the reasons our prayers are so necessary is that God doesn't move without somebody asking Him. Remember when God told Amos, "Indeed the Lord God does nothing without revealing His plans to His servants" (Amos 3:7). Before God moves, He tells someone first. I didn't know this for a long time. I used to think, "O my goodness, look at the state of the priesthood, look at the state of America, look at all those children starving. Why doesn't somebody do something?" I was sitting in the cloister thinking, "Somebody should be out there doing something. You know, God, why don't You do something? You're God. If I were God, I'd do something."

I didn't understand why, but now I know that *we* have to ask. He wants us to ask. Jesus has told us this over and over again, "Ask." "Ask, and you will receive" (Mt 7:7). "All you ask the Father in my name he will give you" (Jn 15:16). That doesn't mean we just say "in the name of Jesus" and get whatever we want, but it means we have a union with Jesus, like women have the names of their husbands because of their union with them. We're talking about a relationship with Jesus that is so intimate that we can go forth and pray in His place, pray in His name and it will be as if Jesus Himself prayed. Jesus has become so enfleshed within us that once again Jesus prays, but this time from deep within us. He desires to pray through us. This is why Jesus wants us to ask because He wants to move again and to bring His people to salvation.

Before we pray, we always need to check it out, "What does the Father want me to do right now?" Just because someone is asking us for prayer does not mean we pray with everyone. Maybe right at that moment we might not know what God is saying. It could be that the Lord is saying for us to set up certain times and certain hours for prayer ministry, to get a structured time frame to pray over people. He doesn't want us to get burned out. One time when we were in Medjugorje, we took our petitions, and the visionaries said they could not take any more prayer requests for two weeks. They said, "We have to rest." Busyness is a powerful and effective tool of Satan. Ministry is a work of God. It is good, but we have to learn to say "no." We can get tired and worn out over anything, even good things.

When I first came out of the cloister, I didn't know how to say "no" unless I had a reason for declining. If somebody wanted me to come to dinner and I didn't want to go for dinner because I was tired, I didn't know how to say, "No, thank you." The Lord showed me that I was in bondage. He said, "Unless you are free enough to say 'no,' then you are not totally free enough to say 'yes' to Me either." So once we hear from the Lord on how to pray and if the Lord is saying "no," then we need to say "no." Once we have heard from the Lord, our obedience to God is key. You'll find that God will never over-tax us. He balances everything in our life beautifully. There can be some days and some weeks when we are in heavy ministry and very busy. We've got a lot of things on our agenda, but this is what God wants and He provides the energies for us to do it. We think, "Look at all I did this past month! This is amazing! Now if I could get this much done every month, this would be great." Then comes the next month and you may hardly accomplish anything because He doesn't want it. You're tired and it's time to rest.

In this type of prayer ministry it is easy to get overwhelmed, but God is right there with us, encouraging us to trust Him and to take the next step in faith. We have received all the gifts necessary for this type of intercessory prayer at Baptism, where we received the gifts of faith, hope, and charity. They will be the means through which the Trinity will work in our lives. We know as baptized Catholics that the Trinity is within us. We are never without the Trinity. So as we embark on this journey, "Do not live in fear, little flock. It has pleased your Father to give you the kingdom" (Lk 12:32). We want to know His voice so well every day, the way He speaks to us personally, so that when we hear the other voices, we will know right away that it's not God and we won't follow.

Although intercessory prayer and contemplative prayer are different, they go together. We need both. Intercessory prayer brings forth the fruit of contemplative prayer. Many times people don't understand that and wonder why their intercession is not effective. Our intercession must come out of our deep union with the Trinity, from our contemplative prayer. This is why our prayers are effective. Intercessory prayer is always directed to the Father. This is why we must know Him. We must have this union. When Jesus taught us to pray, He taught us to pray to the Father, but He taught us to pray with Him, because He is the Way. It is through Him (Jesus), with Him, and in Him that we go to the Father. Intercession is basically to the Father, with, in and through Jesus and through the power of the Holy Spirit. This is Trinitarian prayer.

Chapter 3

Relationship with the Trinity

The Father—the Creator and Deliverer

Being a convert, I didn't always have a relationship with God the Father, but I did have a beautiful relationship with my own father. When I was studying to become a Catholic, I knew that he would not like that, so I took instruction privately. I was going to be baptized on Christmas Eve. My mother had died earlier and my father had remarried and was coming to Omaha to share Christmas with me. I was hoping that this was going to be as beautiful a Christmas present for him as it was for me, but when I told him on Christmas Day that I had become Catholic, he did not like it at all and he disowned me totally. I was crushed! I spent my first twenty-four hours in the Catholic Church trying to make a decision if I was going to stay in the Catholic Church! I said, "Lord, this is a pretty high price." Fathers and daughters can have such a deep relationship, a deep bonding, and since my mother was not living, my father and I were very, very close. He disowned me right there on Christmas Day and when he got home, he wrote a letter to me putting it in writing.

I sat down in a very childish manner, very hurt, and responded with, "Since you're not going to be my father anymore, I'm not going to be your daughter anymore either." For some particular reason, I took my letter to the priest who had just baptized me and I showed it to him and said, "What do you think?" Now that was the first time I'd ever done that. If I had a letter to write, I'd just write it and mail it. The priest sat there and shook his head very slowly, "No." I was on the other side of the desk and I said, "What do you mean?" He said, "I mean we don't send this letter." I said, "Really, what do we do?" He said, "You've been writing to your father every other week.

You continue to write, and basically, you turn the other cheek." I said, "Turn the other cheek? I never heard of that. Who said that?" He answered, "Jesus said that." I asked, "Oh, what does that mean?" He said, "It means you go to church every day and you pray your heart out. You keep loving your father. You write and tell him what you're doing and you never refer to his letter. You just pray and let God handle it."

Little did I know that God the Father was setting up the stage for a whole lifetime of letting God handle it. That's what we have to do. "Father, these people are hurting. They need Your help. Father, You handle it." So for three months I never heard from my father, but I kept writing and I prayed my heart out. Those first months in the Catholic Church I didn't know you could pray for anything other than somebody else! God took me into the ministry of intercession right away because I was driven by love. I was focusing on praying for my father and restoring our relationship. These were prayers from deep down inside my heart. After three months I received a beautiful letter. My father had a dream in which his own father had appeared to him. My father was an only child so he had had a close relationship with his father. This was the authority figure in his life. My grandfather appeared in the dream and said, "Don't worry about Nadine anymore. It's all right. She's a child of God's now." That so impressed my father that he immediately wrote a letter of reconciliation and of acceptance of my Catholic faith.

Through this experience two major things happened to me: I learned the power of prayer of intercession and the power of letting God handle it. The very first thing I ever knew about prayer was to **turn to the Father**. I also came to know and love God the Father during those heart-breaking three months. I so desperately needed a father in my life, so I turned to our Heavenly Father right away and He loved me as I've never been loved before. This relationship with the Father is so important, especially for intercessors.

The Our Father is one of my favorite prayers and I used to sing the Our Father a lot in a croaky, froggy voice. One day I asked the Lord, "What's Your favorite song?" He said, "The Our Father." I asked Him why and He answered, "Because I wrote it." Once as I was preparing to give a talk on the Our Father, I was meditating and pondering on the first two words,

"Our Father." I thought, "Hmmm. Our Father. This is wonderful. We're all together in this now. We're all brothers and sisters. We all have this one Father. He's Our Father." That's where my thoughts were, but then Jesus spoke and He said, "No, we start with Our Father first, *Our* Father. Yes, your Father and My Father, *Our* Father." That's mind boggling! Jesus said, "We have the same Father. When you pray say, 'Our Father' you don't have to go into the presence of the Father by yourself if you don't want to. He's Our Father. Your Father and My Father. He's <u>Our</u> Father. . . and pray that His Kingdom will come." This is what takes place in our prayer. We enter into our prayer with our own agenda, our own self love, very full of the kingdoms of the world, and as we begin to ask the Father, "Let Your Kingdom come now more within me," we will start to experience change. Like the song says, "Change my heart, O God, make it ever true. Change my heart, O God, and make me more like you." That's very much our prayer.

Jesus wants prayer to the Father so much because this was the way He prayed. Jesus prayed to the Father. A relationship with the Father is key to an intercessor, for several reasons. One is that the Father Himself will deliver us and others from the real high-powered evil. Jesus prayed, "Father, deliver us from evil" (Mt 6:13), and so we also pray, "Father, deliver us from evil." Father, deliver us from the evil one now, with Jesus and using Jesus.

The Apostles tried to cast out a demon and they couldn't do it. When they asked Jesus what they did wrong, He said, "This kind you can drive out only by prayer" (Mk 9:14-29). Some Bible translations say, "by prayer and fasting." Did you ever wonder what Jesus meant when He said "this kind?" I used to meditate on that a lot, and I'm sure there are many different theories, but I have come to know in recent years that there is a "this kind" of evil, and it's very, very high powered. The Father alone is the One who can deliver us from "this kind." In fact, just recently, I was praying with somebody via phone, who wanted prayer for an estranged member of her family. When we went into prayer, we discovered that this person was involved in such high powered evil, that the Lord told me, "For this kind, you just ask Me to do it. You stay out of it, and leave it to Me. I'll deliver him." The image that came was of the Father coming and lifting him right out of the flames of hell. So, that's what I mean. There is a "this kind" of evil, and you need the Father to be the Deliverer.

We need a relationship with the Father where we know the Father well, and also a relationship in which we are known by the Father. Jesus tells the woman at the well "Authentic worshipers will worship the Father in Spirit and truth. Indeed, it is just such worshipers the Father seeks" (Jn 4:23). That is so hopeful, that the Father is seeking people like us. He's looking for us. Again, here we are. We want to worship You in Spirit and in truth, but in order to do this we need to go into that inner room daily, especially in the beginning stages of our prayer journey when we don't stand in pure Truth. We have not been purified yet. Most of us don't even know pure Truth. We live in so much deception and are living out of a false self image— we don't even know who we really are, and so it takes time to allow the Kingdom to come within us. God's Light and Truth will come within our hearts and we will slowly be changed. Truth is a Person, the Spirit of God, the Holy Spirit. He is the Spirit of Truth, and He'll remove the falseness within us.

Praying for others can't be helped, really, because when you come into a union with God, whether it be the Father, the Son, or the Holy Spirit, you are going to begin to pick up on what's in Their mind and in Their heart, and it's going to be souls. It's always going to be souls. The desire to bring all people into union with Himself so preoccupies the mind and heart of God at all times. It preoccupies the mind and heart of the Lord so much that They (the Trinity) held that Divine Council and decided that one of Us needs to go to earth and do something so that these souls can come home. The Father said, "I want us to be family again, so that we can be One, and so they can call Me Father." It was decided, as we know, that it would be the Second Person of the Trinity, who at that time was the Word, that would come to earth. "The Word was in God's presence, and the Word was God" (Jn 1:1). That Word, it was decided, would be the Person of the Trinity to become flesh, to become one of us and that's when He took on His human name of Jesus. Jesus' whole life's mission was of the same mind and heart of the Father, in union with Their common Spirit, the Holy Spirit—their mission was for souls. Through Jesus' death on the cross, His Redemption opened the door so that we all could come home.

32

In our intercessory prayer, we need vision. We need the direction of God. In Revelation 4, we read, "Come up here and I will show you what must take place in time to come" (Rv 4:1). Come up here, come up into my presence, come higher, my friend. Come to the mountaintop. Anytime you see in Scripture, "Come up here, come to the mountaintop," you're coming into the presence of God and in that presence, the gift of wisdom begins to work more fully within us and we begin to see through God's eyes. That's how the gift works. We begin to see through God's eyes what He wants and we begin to be directed by Him. We need God's vision! "See, I am doing something new! Now it springs forth, do you not perceive it?" (Is 43:19) This is the gift of understanding that's working at this level. When we come into the presence of God for this direction, we begin to perceive something new. Every time we go to pray, it is something new. We need God's direction. We need to see things from God's point of view.

The vision and the passion together in intercession makes this a very missionary ministry. We can go anywhere in the world with this kind of vision and this kind of power. Intercession primarily takes place between two parties, one being God and the other being man, that man ordinarily being the intercessor. We are speaking directly to God on behalf of someone else or some situation.

This prayer of intercession is the type of prayer that is most feared by Satan because in this type of prayer, God is the One who goes into action. God moves. In many ministries, we move, we do something, we minister to the sick or the poor, we teach in schools, whatever the corporal or spiritual works of mercy are, and they're important, but it very much depends on what *we* do. The ministry of intercession depends solely on what *God does* and this is why it is so feared by Satan, because he is up against his worst enemy. He is brought face to face with God. God moves when we ask Him to. We don't. It is God that goes into action. Our action is simply to ask the Lord to really do it. So, God moves and when He does, many things happen! God reconciles mankind to Himself. God repairs His beautiful work of art, His beautiful human creation.

Jesus is still in the process of redeeming but He needs other human bodies to do it. So He's asking us to allow Him to take up His Cross and live out the fullness of the mystery of the Incarnation again, but this time in us. As we allow this to take place, we enter fully into His ministry, which is intercession. So many times we focus on the ministry of Jesus as one of teaching, healing, deliverance, and all those are true. He was engaged in those ministries. He still seeks and uses people who allow the Word to come forth, who allow His healing power to come forth, the prophetic word, and the wisdom of God, but as St. Paul tells us, "Jesus has obtained a more excellent ministry now" (Heb 8:6). "He forever lives to make intercession for them" (Heb 7:24). Jesus has entered into a far more excellent ministry now, that of intercession at the right hand of the Father and He wants to use us. Isn't that beautiful?!

I used to think that Jesus just sat up there at the right hand of the Father praying for all of us, but that's not exactly how it works. Because He is Jesus, He is still the Word made flesh, but now His intercession takes place when we allow Him to become enfleshed in us. He has access to the Father but this time it's in us, with us, and through us. This is the main thing. Intercession cannot take place except through humanity, except through Jesus and those that allow Jesus to live in them, so He can live out this mystery of Redemption once again. God will not move unless He is asked to move, particularly by His Son, Jesus. Jesus said, "Father, I thank you for having heard me. I know that you always hear me" (Jn 11:42). That's true. So when we allow Jesus to pray within us, through the Spirit of Jesus, we know the Father will always hear our prayer. That is the very heart of intercession. It's prayer at its best because we have access to the throne room of God through Jesus anytime.

Queen Esther is a beautiful example of this. In the Book of Esther in the Old Testament, we see how important it is to have access to the king. One of the great intercessors, Queen Esther, laid her life on the line when she went to the king without an appointment, which meant death. She was a Jewish person married to a non-Jewish person and they were going to put her entire race to death. She went in to see the king anyway, almost fainted, and had to be held up on both sides as she pleaded for her entire race's life to be spared. She asked that their lives be spared even though she knew her life was at stake. It's a beautiful story.

If you haven't read the life of Queen Esther, I would suggest that you read it and note her relationship with the king. You'll see the power that comes forth when you come face to face with the King when you have this kind of intimate relationship, you can ask whatever you will. That's what we're talking about in contemplative prayer—because of the depth of our relationship with the King of kings and the Lord of lords, we know God will hear our prayer. God has shown us His heart, and we simply ask Him to do what He has shown us. So contemplative prayer is essential because it is out of that union that the dynamic of intercession comes. Jesus said, "If you live in me, and my words stay part of you, you may ask what you will—it will be done for you" (Jn 15:7).

Sometimes we may wonder "Why doesn't God answer my prayers?" If this is true, then that's when we have to look at our relationship with Him. What's happening in my day-to-day personal relationship with Him? Am I making contact? Is there that union? Oftentimes we find there can be a subtle fear preventing us from coming this close to Jesus because He's going to ask me to change. Heaven forbid that God would ask me to change! Also the thought that my prayers could actually be answered might be kind of scary, so what do we do in response? All of a sudden, before we even realize it, we run.

The way I used to run from this union with God would be talking extra long on the telephone. I had one phone conversation after the other, so I was really too busy to pray very much. Some of us can get into good books and can read and read wonderful things about Jesus, but we never really get into the one-on-one, "You and me" relationship. That's running. We all have our ways of doing this and if we find that we are living a lifestyle that we're not totally comfortable with, one of the first places it's going to show up is in our prayer life. We're not going to want to spend too much time with Someone who has that x-ray vision and can see into our hearts. We'll run because He might penetrate right through all of my masks and really say, "Let's talk about this." "Come now, let us set things right, says the Lord: Though your sins be like scarlet, they may become white as snow" (Is 1:18). He's saying, "It's okay, but let's talk about it." So we have to be careful that we're not running from God. We want Jesus to continue His wonderful ministry of coming before the Father with, in, and through us today.

I think this is amazing that God is this dependent upon us to move. In one sense, He's almost as helpless now as when He was a baby at Bethlehem. Sometimes I wonder how much more God would be moving in the world and in people's lives if we were asking Him to move. We have an assumption, "Well, You're God. You know all these things. You know the situation. You know what's going to happen. You don't need me to pray. You have the power to do something about it. If I were God and I saw that something was going to happen, I would go ahead and prevent it. I would just do it." That's our mentality, particularly as Americans because we know how to fix everything. We're doers. We think, "I can't see why God just doesn't fix everything. He's got the power. He's got the knowledge. He knows what to do far better than we do." But you see, Jesus is His intercessor and He waits for the Jesus in each of us to ask Him, and if He doesn't get asked, He doesn't move. God does not move without being asked.

It is absolutely essential in any quality prayer to learn to listen to what **God** wants to say **to us**. Once we pick up the mind and heart of God in any situation, that means that God is ready to move in that situation. It means, "I'm going to do it. This is what I want you to ask Me. Ask Me now." It's that simple. That's the dynamic.

I was listening to a tape by a non-Catholic with a dynamic ministry in another city and they had decided that they were going to pray for a revival in their church in this particular city. They prayed and prayed for these conversions—month after month after month and nothing happened. Finally the leader was in his private prayer, and the Lord told him then, "I want you to ask Me what's in My heart right now." So he said, "Okay Lord, what's in Your heart?" And the Lord told him what was in His heart and told him, "Now, ask Me to do just what I showed you was in My heart and in My mind." This just overwhelmed him! We wonder, "Lord why don't You just do it? You know what's in Your mind and in Your heart. Why do you tell me that I have to ask You to do it before you do it?" And the answer is because God only works through humanity, because He's Jesus. He is the Intercessor at the right hand of the Father and He only works through humanity.

So these people had no idea what God wanted them to pray for until the leader learned this very simple principle of intercessory prayer. The Lord didn't want them to pray the way they were praying at all. He said this isn't in My mind or in My heart right now. I want you to pray about another situation instead, and they did, and they saw tremendous fruit come forth from their intercessory prayer.

Sr. Ann Shields tells the story about a group of ladies that attended a FIRE rally in Ohio, who had heard this principle on intercessory prayer for the first time. For three years, they had been praying that an abortion clinic would close, and yet all it seemed to do was flourish. They prayed and prayed that the owner would close the clinic because obviously it was God's will. On the way home from the rally they were discussing this and one lady said that maybe they should check with the Lord to make sure that the prayer they had been praying was the prayer He wanted prayed. Another lady said, "Of course God wants this abortion clinic closed. We know His will." A third lady said, "Why don't we just ask God if we're honestly praying in His name."

So they finally all agreed that they would pray, "Lord if You want to change our prayer, we can't imagine that You do, but if You want to change or adjust anything, let us know." All of a sudden, their car was filled with tremendous light and instantly they all knew how to pray. "We are to pray for the conversion of the owner." They were amazed and this was how they prayed. One month later, the owner was converted and he closed the abortion clinic! One month after praying for three years! What a loving God that He wants to reach out in love to all people! Now they understood this whole principle of asking God to reveal His heart and mind to us. So it is very important to try and find out how the Lord wants us to pray. That's why contemplative prayer, being in the listening mode, is so important. If we don't learn how to listen to God, we can pray about a situation for a long time, and usually we'll end up frustrated. Our way of praying might not be exactly what God wants us to pray so we don't always bear the fruit from our prayers that we would like to bear. Jesus desires to become enfleshed once again, but this time within us. *Jesus* is the Intercessor.

The Holy Spirit—the Power

The Holy Spirit is the power. He is holy. Mary talks about Him in her Magnificat, "Holy is his name" (Lk 1:49). His name is Holy. He comes and dwells within us, and calls us into that relationship of holiness within Himself.

One of the main ministries of the Holy Spirit is to transform us into the very image of God Himself, of Jesus Christ. It's a beautiful mystery that God actually dwells within us and that He can dwell more fully within us each day as we open ourselves in that beautiful surrender to His overshadowing Spirit, to His power. Jesus was always led by the Holy Spirit: led out of Nazareth, led into the desert, led back out of the desert, led into different ministries, led to Calvary, and then led on into Heaven. We, too, must always be led and directed by the Holy Spirit. This is what will make our intercession effective—that the Holy Spirit is leading and teaching us at all times, just as He led and taught Jesus.

We might ask ourselves, "Just what is intercession?" It is prayer that is directed and energized by the Holy Spirit for others. "The Spirit too helps us in our weakness, for we do not know how to pray as we ought; but the Spirit himself makes intercession for us with groanings that cannot be expressed in speech. He who searches hearts knows what the Spirit means, for the Spirit intercedes for the saints as God himself wills" (Rom 8:26-27).

In Baptism the Holy Spirit comes to us right away and we have the empowerment of the Holy Spirit. It's one thing to know what God wants us to pray about, but then we need that power of the Holy Spirit in order for that prayer to be effective. God wants us to experience His Love, the divine presence of the Trinity· within us and the great weapon that Love is. I didn't always understand that we really have the same Holy Spirit as Jesus Christ. It's amazing! I thought, "Well, yes, we have the Holy Spirit, but He (Jesus) had **The** Holy Spirit. All that knowledge, all that understanding." Well, we might not have the Holy Spirit in the same fullness that Jesus had, but we have the *same* Spirit leading us and directing us.

This was quite a revelation to me when I really began to understand that this is the same Holy Spirit leading us that led Jesus. It helped me to really trust the Holy Spirit. I told Him, "You didn't make a mistake with Jesus. Hopefully, You're not going to make a mistake with me either." It's beautiful that we're led by the Spirit because He is the Spirit of Light. "God is Light; in him there is no darkness" (1Jn 1:15). The Paraclete "is the Spirit of truth who comes from the Father" (Jn 15:26).

We will also be energized by the Holy Spirit. The Holy Spirit, the Sanctifier, brings us seven gifts. These are the Isaiah gifts that we all received at Confirmation and were given to us for our own personal growth in holiness. "The spirit of the Lord shall rest upon him; a spirit of wisdom and of understanding, a spirit of counsel and of strength, a spirit of knowledge and of fear of the Lord, and his delight shall be the fear of the Lord" (Is 11:2-3). These seven gifts of the Holy Spirit are given to each person for their own personal sanctification to become a saint.

Fear of the Lord is a beautiful gift. It enables us to become righteous and sinless through a deep hatred for sin. We desire to only do what pleases the Father. We cling to God with tremendous reverence. This gift helps us in the purification process because it encourages the emptying of self, with a desire for more and more of God.

The gift of **Counsel** is where the Spirit constantly counsels us, showing us what to do, what not to do. Counsel enlightens the mind, directs and guides us in every circumstance. "I will counsel you, keeping my eye on you" (Ps 32:8). This spirit of counsel will help us to make good decisions. "While from behind, a voice shall sound in your ears; 'This is the way; walk in it" (Is 30:21).

The gift of **Knowledge** is working so that we have insight into Who God is and who we are. This is a knowledge of holy things and the things that God made. Knowledge enables us to put on the mind of Jesus Christ, thereby entering into His "sonship" and into our true identity as children of God. We start to experience a second conversion because Truth is so great that it empties out all within us that is not of God.

The gift of **Fortitude** is so necessary in our every day living because we really need courage to allow God to continue His purification work within us. Fortitude gives us the tremendous strength of the Spirit Himself. This will help us as intercessors because we will become stronger and sacrifices will become easier for us.

The gift of **Piety** makes us concerned about the honor and glory of the Father because we are His children. We view God as Father. We give thanks to God not because He made us or because of the benefits we receive, but for the glory and honor of the Father. As this gift operates more fully within us, we start to be unified together as brothers and sisters in Christ. We identify with our brothers and sisters to the point where we are willing to lay down our life for them.

The gift of **Understanding** reveals hidden things. We will start to understand human events from God's point of view. This is a special gift for contemplatives because by means of understanding, we go deep into the meaning of the supernatural truths of the Christian mysteries. For example, we will begin to understand the doctrine of the Eucharist, which is beyond human understanding or our knowledge. We will thirst for holiness and our souls, united to God, will know Him by a direct, sweet experience.

The gift of **Wisdom** is the gift of gifts. This gift makes us friends with God. Jesus is Wisdom Incarnate and the more Wisdom resides in us, the more we reflect Jesus to the Father. The more we reflect Jesus to the Father, the more powerful our prayer will be. Wisdom gives our souls the power to experience divine things. It enables us to put on the Lord Jesus Christ.

At the first Pentecost, we see the Holy Spirit moving in tremendous power. The disciples were told to prepare for this kind of power and to wait for it until they were clothed with power from on high (Acts 1: 4-8). Even the early Church was in desperate need of the power of the Holy Spirit. They waited and waited. They didn't know how long it would take for this empowerment but they just knew that they were told to wait, so they did.

We also want to be clothed with power from on high. We want to be filled with the fire of His Love. We want to be filled with the Holy Spirit every day. There was an actual moment in time where in the Upper Room the Holy Spirit descended, but the Upper Room for us today is not a place but it is very much the higher faculties of our soul. It's in our will. It's in all the faculties so we can choose, so we can know, so we can understand. We need this constant Life every day. We need Pentecost every day.

The children of God are to be led by the Spirit of God. This is extremely important for us to remember at all times. We think we will never forget that we are to be led by the Spirit of God, but in the practical, day-to-day living, we do forget. We are not accustomed to constantly being led by the Divine Spirit. He is so gentle so we have to be very perceptive and very aware of His movement. We must listen and wait for it. The beauty of being led by the Holy Spirit, when we really understand it, is that God will never lead us into any kind of danger. He will never lead us into any kind of evil or anything that would be sin. He's pure. He is the Holy One. His movement and His leading will always lead us towards God, always.

We should never move on out without the empowerment of the Holy Spirit. There are times when we feel we don't have His power which can be the movement of God, too. It means "wait." Without the Holy Spirit we do not have the power to move on out. We don't have the direction, we don't have the light, we don't have the discernment. He is the Spirit of Truth and Wisdom and He comes with many gifts. Without the Holy Spirit, we don't move at all, and so we need to learn to wait. A lot of good things can happen when we wait on the Lord, but most of all, in our waiting we learn to trust Him and believe His word to us. God never misses on His timing.

Another ministry of the Spirit is to sanctify us, to make us holy, and to transform us into the perfect image of Jesus. The Holy Spirit will work with us and purify us. He's very gentle. He will sanctify us if we allow Him to take us through the purification process. We have many saints in the Catholic Church who have made this journey themselves. Two saints in particular, Teresa of Avila and John of the Cross have written a lot about the purification process. We are body, soul and spirit and we have to be purified at all three levels because we lost all of that in the Fall in the Garden. The only gift we did not lose was the gift of our free will to choose. It's a beautiful ministry of the Spirit. We can always choose to accept God's leading or not. St. Paul talks about this purification as the "Ministry of the Spirit." We go from glory to glory, from one level to another and another, as more and more Light comes into us and more and more darkness leaves us. We're being cleansed: more of God, less of me. Hopefully He will begin to increase in all of us.

St. Iraneus said, "Man fully alive is the glory of God" (*Against Heresies*, Book IV). When we really ponder "to be fully alive," we have to look to Jesus because Jesus tells us "I am the way, and the truth, and the life" (Jn 14:6). So if we want to be "fully alive," if we want to reflect the glory of God, then we have to be full of Life Himself, we have to be full of Jesus. This is the Ministry of the Spirit: to take us from glory to glory to glory until we are filled with God's glory, filled with God's Life. "All of us, gazing on the Lord's glory with unveiled faces, are being transformed from glory to glory into his very image by the Lord who is the Spirit" (2 Cor 3:18). We're fully alive. This is why Jesus came—that we could have this Life and have it in abundance (Jn 10:10).

The tendency and temptation in this purification process is to hide. It's a stripping process, and Adam and Eve tried to hide their sins from God, and they hid. God was walking with them in the Garden every day and now all of a sudden, they're hiding. God asks, "Where are you?" (Gn 3:9) Well, this is what He is always saying to us, "Where are you?" It's like the beautiful stars in the Heaven. He put them in place and said, "Where are you?" and they answered, "Here we are! shining with joy for (our) Maker" (Bar 3:35). He wants us to shine like the stars. He wants us to be bright and full of Light.

So we have to reveal ourselves in our sinfulness to God. We can't hide it. We've all gone to a doctor so he can help us. He may ask, "Show me where it hurts." Imagine our reply being, "I can't do that." He'd have to answer, "Well, if I can't see the wound, how am I going to treat it?" Sometimes we are this way with the Divine Physician. We try to hide our true, sinful condition from Him, and we think, "It's just a little thing, He won't notice. He won't even see it." Sometimes we're not even aware that we are covering up.

One of the beautiful things about being led and directed by the Sanctifier, the Holy Spirit, on this beautiful path of Love is that it always keeps us in this posture of being little like children. Following is for children. One time the Lord gave me an image of heaven and, honestly, I couldn't believe it! It was nothing but a nursery, babies, babies everywhere, but He was trying to make a point—you've got to change. There has to be a conversion process going on within. "Trust me when I tell you that whoever does not accept the kingdom of God as a child will not enter into it" (Lk 18:17). So we want to allow ourselves to become like children and enjoy being emptied by the Holy Spirit. Anything He wants to remove from us, He will give back a hundredfold, believe me. God will never be outdone in generosity.

St. Paul tells us, "God's kindness is an invitation to you to repent" (Rom 2:4). We won't really be willing to change until we start to feel loved, and the Holy Spirit *is* Love. So we first need to experience God's Love in order to have the strength and courage to begin this process of purification. That's why the Holy Spirit is the Sanctifier. He wants to transform us into the image of Jesus. He is such a Spirit of Love, pure Love. So we first need to experience His Love. Jesus and the Father first establish a relationship with us, to where we begin to feel loved and secure in Their presence. Once we feel comfortable and loved, the Holy Spirit will slowly call us and encourage us to repent and change. We will begin to start looking at ourselves in God's Light, and the Holy Spirit will slowly reveal to us more and more of who we are. Because we're believing in God's love for us, we won't be so fearful that we're going to lose Love or endanger our relationship with the Trinity, and we'll be able to embark upon this journey of purification.

As a child, whenever I went out the door, my daddy used to say, "Now, be a good little girl. Come straight home." When I became a Catholic and met God the Father, I thought that's exactly what the Heavenly Father wants. He wants us to be good, like Him, but only God is good. Jesus said to the rich man, "Why do you call me good? No one is good but God alone" (Mk 10:18). Jesus is God, too, but Jesus wasn't revealing this at that time. So now the Father is saying to us, "I want you to be holy. I want you to be like Me. I want you to be good, and

I want you to come straight home. None of this Purgatory stuff, straight home." Well, this is one of the ways we can get there— we can allow the Sanctifier to take us through the conversion process. He will, if we will let Him. God will never violate our free will, He will not go against our wishes. He's so gentle. He will let us choose.

So first the Father formed us, then we kind of got de-formed through sin, and now the Holy Spirit comes alone and is re-forming us, informing us, and hopefully, transforming us! This is the whole sanctifying process. There's many things that happen in this process, but one of the main things that happens is that as we walk more and more in His Light, we get to know God and we start to know who we are in His Light. "God is Spirit," (Jn 4:24) the Holy Spirit is the Spirit of Light (1Jn 1:5). We will begin to see some of our flaws, some of our imperfections, some of the hidden things and faults in the recesses of our heart. We can bring these flaws into His Love for Him to cleanse and purify. His interest is in our purity, our holiness, our wholeness, our being totally surrendered and full of God. That's sanctity and this is what God desires.

There are a few movements of the heart where we will begin to pick up in prayer at this level that will help with discernment. The heart is very much the discerner here, and the movement of the Holy Spirit within the heart is how we learn good discernment. God has already equipped us, but we need to know it to use it. We need the gift of Knowledge to know God, but also to know myself. Each day St. Augustine would pray, "To know you my God and to know myself." It is a gift of God to be led by the Holy Spirit. In the early Church, they were constantly led by the Holy Spirit, "It is the decision of the Holy Spirit, and ours too. . ." (Acts 15:28). How much easier choices can be when we're making them together with the Holy Spirit.

The movement of the Holy Spirit within our lives will always move us toward God, always. The fruit of the Holy Spirit will be deeper union with God. St. Paul tells us, "At every opportunity, pray in the Spirit" (Eph 6:18). We pray in the Spirit, with the Spirit, and we are constantly being led by the Spirit. "May he strengthen you inwardly through the working of his Spirit" (Eph 3:16).

In summary, intercession is primarily **to the Father, in union with Jesus**, and it is always **in the power of the Holy Spirit**. Intercession is Trinitarian; Jesus prayed to the Father and our intercession has its power in this union with, in, and through Jesus. Jesus is the center. With, in, and through Jesus we come into this friendship, into that childhood and have, then, this relationship with the Father. This is what gives our prayer its power. All this happens in this love power of the Holy Spirit. Intercession is the fullness of our Baptismal Gift when we received the Trinity.

Chapter 4

Agape Intercession:
Called to be Burden Bearers

At Baptism we each received three precious gifts: faith, hope, and charity. Of course, they came in seed form as most of God's gifts do. They start out dormant within us until we become conscious and aware of them and start to use them. As we use these gifts, they start to blossom and grow. We will never exhaust the many, many different dimensions of these gifts or use them in their entirety. God is so good that He has given us all we need on this journey. He is always calling us to a deeper union with Him and to be more like His Son each day and He has equipped us with these gifts of **faith, hope,** and **love** to enable us to do this. Intercessors become aware of these Baptismal gifts early in their ministry because we need them, and it is through their use that these gifts grow and mature.

As we start to reach out for others in prayer, we find that our gift of **faith** grows. We can believe that God is right there and that He cares for us. The gift of **hope** develops very quickly because as we stand "bridging the gap" between God and man we find we need hope as we will come into suffering a great deal. When one is suffering, one starts to hope in God, and if nothing else, we hope that it will end! Then we come into this great gift of **love** which is the focus of this chapter.

Agape Love
The type of love that we are referring to is called **"agape"** love. It is a very special type of love; it is Calvary love. Jesus' prayers were answered through His sacrifice. It is through Jesus' dying to self and allowing Himself to be crucified that His

prayers had power. When we pray, we also need this kind of love power.

Remember when Jesus asked Peter, "Do you love me?" (Jn 21:15) Well yes, Peter did love Him. Along with Peter we can say, "Yes, Lord, I love You." But then Jesus asked him again, "Simon, son of John, do you love me?" (Jn 21:16) Greek scholars say that the word Jesus used for love was "Agape" meaning a deep sacrificial love. Peter's response "yes Lord, You know I love You" used another word "philo," for love meaning the kind of love that we love as brothers and friends. "Do you agape me, Peter?" "Yes, Lord, I philo You." But the third time that Jesus asked him that question, "Do you love me?" (Jn 21:17), He changed "philo" for the word "agape." "Do you philo me, Peter?" Peter was grieved. He was distressed, and said, "Lord, you know everything. You know well that I love (philo) you" (Jn 21:17). By this time Peter has learned humility. He's speaking truth. He knows Jesus knows all things. "Lord, You know all things, and You know that I philo You." That's truth. Peter knew that he wanted to say "Yes I agape You" but he also knew he wasn't quite there yet. That's humility. If this is where we are, "Lord, I philo You," that's where we are. It's okay with the Lord. We may not be able to say, "Lord, I agape You. I'll lay down my life for You and for Your people," but it is okay. Wherever we are at, this is the point from which our journey begins. God desires our heart to be open to Him; He can do the rest.

So we may not have love at the same level that we saw Queen Esther was at. We may not be ready to give our life for God's people. But as we grow in the use these gifts of faith, hope, and love, and come to trust in them, we may be asked at different times in intercession to lay down our lives for our people, for our Church, for our families, for our neighbors, maybe even for our enemies in our intercessory prayer. To do this we need love power from the Holy Spirit, and we receive it simply by asking. It comes from the desire. All gifts come from desiring them. If we don't even want these gifts, then we pray and ask for the desire to want them.

For example, when we pray with people for forgiveness, many times the gift of forgiveness doesn't come. It's not that our prayers aren't answered but it may be because they don't want it. Often people don't desire to forgive because they're still in too much pain, so we have to minister to the pain first. So we ask God to give them a desire to at least want to forgive and when that desire starts to be kindled within a soul, then the gift will come. As intercessors, as prayer warriors, we need to desire this type of agape love if we don't already have it. "Lord, I can't hold all these people and concerns within my own heart. It's too small and too selfish. Lord, please replace my heart with Your heart of love."

Amazingly we have already received this deep level of love, this gift of agape love, at Baptism. It is love that brings forth Jesus' power. Jesus said, "I have power to lay it (my life) down" (Jn 10:18). This deep sacrificial love takes a tremendous amount of love. We need this kind of love. Jesus is our model of how we are to be. "There is no greater love than this: to lay down one's life for one's friends" (Jn 15:13). It takes that kind of love and sacrifice, to the point of laying down one's life, to bring forth the power of the Holy Spirit.

"The Office of Intercession"

Intercessors are being called to "The Office of Intercession," which is this deep level of Calvary love. We are being called to stand at the foot of the Cross with Our Lady and intercede along with her. We will be asked to lay down our lives, and the way we are asked to do this will be different for each and every person. We will be asked to sacrifice in the way that can bring the most glory to God.

This sacrifice will be paid in different ways. Those standing at the foot of the Cross with Jesus were paying a tremendous price, and we'll never know the cost to Our Lady. We'll never know what kind of suffering it must have been to have watched Jesus suffer like He did; it took tremendous love power. When we are at this level of agape intercession, we will be experiencing the very pain of God. It will be the Spirit of God within us that is weeping and praying so deeply. We have no idea of the pain and the cost of a soul. All we know is that we get glimpses of the cost through this prayer of Calvary.

St. Paul tells us, "We do not know how to pray as we ought. But the Spirit Himself makes intercession for us with groanings that cannot be expressed" (Rom 8:26). With groanings! That's the Spirit and the Church in travail. That's intercession at its best; that's Calvary intercession, carrying burdens in our whole life. It's a lifestyle. It's not mouthing prayer, but it is feeling the weight of sin, feeling the burden in the heart of Jesus Christ, because His heart is beating within our heart, and we will have ministry at that level of travail.

You have to really be there involved in this prayer to begin to understand this kind of agape love. We all know people who have lost a loved one who never get over it. The pain is too great that they never totally heal. I think there is love at the level where we will only heal when we see them again in heaven. Maybe we're not meant to be totally healed of that kind of loss here. Pain and suffering are part of God's plan, so, there will be tears at times and there will be pain.

Transferences

There can be a price tag in praying for others. In this kind of intercession there are what we call "transferences." This is where God will transfer part of the heavy load from one person that is hurting to an intercessor who is willing to bear the weight for another for awhile. Simon of Cyrene did this for Jesus when he helped carry the Cross, and we are asked to do it, too.

When I was still in the cloister, my room was on the third floor. There was a sister on the second floor who was running a dangerously high fever. One night a couple of nuns came to visit us. It was the first time we heard about the healing ministry and about the gifts of the Holy Spirit. As I walked these nuns to the door, I asked, "I don't know if you have time to stop and see one of our sisters. She's very sick and has a high fever." One of the sisters said, "She'll be well by morning." Deep down I felt the Lord truly was saying this but after they left, I forgot about it.

About 4:00 AM I woke up burning with fever. I had never had a high fever so I didn't even know what it would be like, but right away the Lord was there and said, "It will be okay. This is a transference. I'm healing her." By 6:00 a.m. when everybody was up and around, I was fine and she was fine. I don't think she even knew there was a transference, but that's how God

49

chose to heal her. My health was good, my body was strong, and He wanted me to carry some of the burden for her. God can do whatever He wants and a lot of us have stronger bodies and we can take on things for others. Some have stronger spirits, stronger psyches, and they can take on other people's sins and illnesses without hurting themselves.

This is where a lot of intercessors turn back and decide, "I don't think this ministry is for me." I've told the Lord many times, "It's no wonder You have so few intercessors. It's such an ugly ministry. It's so full of pain. It's so full of sin." And it is. When Jesus took our sin upon Himself, there was a transference that took place. He took **our sin** upon **Himself** so that we could be healed and brought to everlasting life. Jesus continues His intercessory role now but this time within us. Jesus carried our sins, and now we are also called to carry sin for others. You know how much we hate our own sin. Sin is ugly at every level, in every form, that we can't wait to get rid of it.

Purifying the Intercessor

Even though intercessors pray for graces for others, at the same time we're also dealing with our own sins. We're not that sinless Lamb like Jesus was, but we're trying. We're in the process of becoming pure. The Lord will always teach us how to proceed in each case and take us to another level, deeper and deeper, healing the wounds of others while healing the wounds within the intercessor personally. Intercessors go from level to level to level as God begins to trust us more as He sees our faithfulness. God calls us into a ministry like this to take on other people's sin in addition to our own, to carry their burdens for them for awhile so they can be free to receive and accept graces.

So at this level of intercession, it can be like doing double-duty at times: carrying other people's sins while still trying to eliminate our own. This is why the helmet of salvation is so essential; we must **know** that God loves each one of us personally at a very deep level. Our minds must be cleared of negativity, anger, rebellion, resentment, and all those emotions that can tear us away from God, or else when the transference of sin comes, we will not be strong enough to fight it.

Transferences usually will involve our emotions. Have you ever gotten up in the morning feeling very irritable and naturally speaking, you don't have any reason to be irritable? We used to say, "I guess I got up on the wrong side of the bed." Well maybe we did, but maybe we didn't. Maybe God is using us and we are in intercession. Whenever we feel that we may be in intercession for something or for someone, we must always first treat it as if it is our own sin. Otherwise, we can say, "Oh, I can act this way because I'm in intercession," and use it as an excuse for our behavior. "I'm sorry I was so crabby. I think I was in intercession." We have to be careful not to do that. Just because we're in intercession doesn't give us a reason to be uncharitable.

So first we treat this burden as our own sin and take action against it as though it were our own. If it is our own personal sin, we'll come out the better for it. If it's somebody else's sin that we are carrying, we'll both come out better for it. We can only win when we're dealing with decreasing sin! This burden, this emotion or sin, will actually be placed upon us and the transference itself will often tell us how to pray. If you're angry and you don't see the connection to your life at the time, you can almost be sure somebody is angry and needs to be released from this kind of anger. The quicker we can recognize that emotion, bring it to God, and pray for that grace to come to whoever needs it, the sooner they will be healed. Whatever we are experiencing for them will be lifted sooner from us, also, and we will be less likely to fall into that sin ourselves. If we don't pray for that grace for them, then we're going to struggle with that anger ourselves and all of a sudden, if we're not careful, it can become our own personal anger, and we'll lash out at somebody and sin ourselves.

For some reason we seem to be living in a very angry culture, a very angry nation. I don't know when I've ever been aware of so much anger at so many levels. Intercessors can experience anger at many different levels, and it can take all the energies you've got just to be nice when you're feeling this way, but don't give in to it. You want to deal with it and pray for whomever it is that lives in that kind of anger. Once you obtain that grace for someone, you will know it almost immediately because that emotion lifts from you. It just lifts almost as quickly as it came. When we're dealing with our own emotions and sin, it doesn't lift that easily. We have to work it through.

As intercessors, we carry our own emotions and can at times carry transferences of other people's emotions as well. It happens so naturally that sometimes we can't tell the difference. We may wonder, "Is this my real feelings or is this someone else's?" We can ask a prayer partner or somebody in a prayer group to pray for us because we need to know if we're in intercession or not. It makes a big difference to us if we know we're in intercession and not just dealing with our own personal sin. It does help to know. This is why it's always good to be in contact with someone who understands this kind of ministry. We need support.

Once we know that we're in intercession, we start praying, "God, please give them the grace to get out of this! Please give it to them." One time I was on my way to noon Mass, and the priest at the parish said, "By the way, Sister, would you pray for me?" I said, "Certainly, Father." I got in the car and started lifting him up in prayer, "Please help him, dear God, whatever he needs." He hadn't told me what he wanted me to pray for. I was driving in familiar surroundings, I think I could have almost driven it blindfolded, but I missed the turn and ended up going in circles. It took awhile to get back on the freeway. I thought, "Isn't this strange? This has never happened before. I missed a turn. Something must have been confusing me."

Now I'm back driving in circles so I can get back on the interstate again and that's when the light came, "The priest that just asked you to pray is in confusion. He is going in circles." The Lord showed me that he needed to make an important decision. So, there was a transference—I had his confusion, but while I was going in circles, he was able to think clearly, get his discernment, and he made a wonderful decision! This is called "being the victim of your own intercession." I was able to carry the confusion for this priest for a brief while so that he could get that light and direction from the Lord.

We have transferences happen all the time. Transferences are not only in our emotions, they can also be physical transferences. Somebody might get a headache for no reason. A headache can be very symbolic of the crown of thorns which Jesus wore to combat the sin of pride. So we pray, "Lord, whoever is struggling with pride, please give them the humility to say 'yes' to You, to surrender their lives to You." And the more we pray, the more God's graces come, and hopefully someone out there has received the graces to surrender more completely to the Father's will for them, and then the headache goes away!

There is a price on every soul. St. Paul said, "You have been purchased, and at a price" (1Cor 6:20). Paul had an insight into the cost, the tremendous price of a soul. There is a price on every healing and we, as intercessors, are to be like Jesus and say "yes" to carrying some of the burden with Him. We are to be part of the answer to our own intercession, even though it may involve suffering. Often our suffering may be the whole answer to bring forth healing and sometimes it will only be part of the answer.

The transference will cause an intercessor to struggle in whatever area God wants him to be strengthened in. For example, if the prayer is going to free someone from his anger, then that will be what the intercessor will be struggling with himself in his own personal life. The intercessor will willingly accept the struggle and once he sees a change in himself where he is managing his anger better, gaining territory in that area, he will know, "I've got it." Once he gains that intercessory territory and has wrestled with those same issues himself successfully, then anytime he needs to pray in that area for anyone or anything, having already won the battle within himself, the graces will come.

The Lord will always guide us and teach us how to proceed in each case. As we progress in holiness, He will take us to another level, deeper and deeper, healing the wounds of others while healing the wounds within ourselves. We might carry these burdens for others for a short period of time because we are victim lambs of the Lord. As Mary instructed the waiters at the wedding feast of Cana, "Do whatever he tells you" (Jn 2:5), she is encouraging us also, "Follow and accept whatever He gives you so that the life-giving water that He nourishes us with will soon turn into the body and blood of Christ." Our offering, our willingness to carry burdens for others, laying down our lives, can bring forth the dying and rising of Christ again but in others. We are letting Him do whatever He wants.

We have given Him our "yes," but we won't be in the trenches day in and day out. We will get a break! But what will come forth within us from carrying others' burdens is a compassion for the people who actually live in this type of bondage to sin constantly. It will motivate us to pray for their release, for their peace. We can see how heavy a burden sin can be in someone's life when we are carrying their load for awhile. We can see how it is terribly difficult for a person to feel like they want to love God or anybody else if they're feeling this heaviness and darkness. So God releases these heavy burdens from them, asks us to carry it for a while until the graces of peace come to them and they can get their lives back in order. There is no need to fear.

Depression is a difficult transference because we always think it's our own. We question ourselves, "Where did this come from? Do I have some kind of repressed anger? Didn't I get my own way? Did somebody step on my toe? What's going on?" We kind of look at ourselves and question, "Am I getting enough rest? Am I eating right? Am I being faithful to prayer?" This is good—we always need to check out the basics within ourselves first, but when we find that we're okay, we can almost always arrive at the conclusion that we're carrying somebody else's depression. We can feel that burden and heavy darkness. We carry this a lot right now and I'm sure that intercessors in other areas of the country do, too, because the suicide rate is so high. There is tremendous depression, discouragement, and lack of hope within our country. Intercessors can feel this as a transference, and will carry the burden for others, praying for those graces for them to get out from under this terrible bondage. The darkness will start to lift, they will begin to experience God's love, and the healing process will begin. This is good news!

The heaviest burden that gets laid upon intercessors is pride. We are coming against this a lot because this is the sin of all sins. Pride can be manifested in rebellion, anger, spiritual pride, and is part of all the seven capital sins (pride, greed, envy, anger, lust, gluttony, and sloth). Pride can be subtle sometimes. It takes tremendous virtue and energies of an intercessor to really be obedient, to be little, to remain hidden and vulnerable when being assaulted by the emotion of pride. When we're carrying

54

the sin of pride, everything within us wants to strike back and be aggressive, terribly assertive, demanding, and obnoxious. This is a very difficult burden to carry for others as it is also very much within ourselves—in our minds, psyches, spirits, and even our bodies. So when we are carrying pride, the load can be quite heavy.

The Little Flower experienced transferences a lot. She said God would put her in a dark tunnel so others could have light. Whenever she was in that dark tunnel she knew that she was going to come out of it so she didn't need to be afraid. She also knew that whoever she was experiencing this darkness for, whoever's load she was lightening, was going to come out of it, too, because she was interceding and obtaining graces and light for them through her sacrifices. St. Therese said, "For is there a *joy* greater than that of suffering out of love for You? I am in a hole just like that, body and soul. Ah! What darkness! However, I am still at peace. Everything I have, everything I merit, is for the good of the Church and for souls" (*Story of a Soul*, p. 26, 214, 266).

The thing about these transferences that you have to be careful of is that they are very natural so they may not be noticeable; you may not be aware that they are even transferences. Transferences are usually tailor-made to you. For example, fatigue—some of us just sort of drag around all of the time. If there's a transference of fatigue, we may not even recognize it and may not realize that we are to pray. The only thing we may know is that we're a little more tired than normal, but we underestimate fatigue sometimes. When we are tired it can really hurt us if it's not taken care of, because what does it affect first? Our prayer. We cannot pray when we are tired. We can put in the time praying and fall sound asleep. We can escape into the TV set, the telephone, our conversations, or our work because if we keep busy, we'll stay awake. Fatigue can be a tremendous enemy and so God gives these transferences of fatigue to intercessors who will fight it and pray for the graces to counteract it.

Intercession Becomes a Lifestyle

Intercession becomes a way of life. It becomes a lifestyle. We have given our "yes" to God: "Here I am. Use me any way You want to use me." We will be used as a burden bearer because of our willingness to be used in a particular situation so that His love can reach out to a soul and bring it to salvation. God will do His part by pouring out His love upon us in abundance, showering us with the graces we will need to persevere and carry this burden as He did upon Jesus. We can trust God—we **know** that He will be with us. We just give our perpetual "yes" and let the Lord pace us. He won't let us become overextended. If we are checking things out with God, God will see that we are in intercession only when He wants us in intercession. There will be days and days, or even weeks for certain people, when they will not be in any intercession. We do not intercede every day. We may intercede every day for a week or two and then God pulls us back to rest. Resting with God is key. We rest in His love and get recreated ourselves and become even more effective instruments of His love. God believes in rest; He even rested, so we are to rest with Him. This rest is where we get renewed.

At this level of love, we are entering into the redemptive Baptism of Jesus. This is where the Spirit will lead us. The Little Flower said the way of faith is the way of the cross. It's a suffering path. It is strewn with beautiful roses, but all roses have a few thorns. When you get that grace for someone else and the transference lifts, there is just no joy like it! Through our prayers, the person or situation will always get the grace that's needed, but the grace may not always be accepted.

God will give us His plan. When things get overwhelming, He'll dig us out. He'll show us how to delegate, how to appoint. He'll bring forth other people to pray. He's got friends out there! When I was being called out of the cloister and I said, "But Lord, I don't know anybody out there. Who's going to help me with all this?" He said, "I've got friends out there, Nadine. Not your friends, but My friends." We have to trust that.

Victim Lambs

St. Peter said that we are a consecrated people, a holy people, a royal priesthood. If we really believe that we are priestly people, and we are, then doesn't it also mean we have a priestly mission, a priestly ministry? Did you ever think about that? Or did you think it's only for the priests who have the office of priesthood, the ordained priesthood. What about us? What about this priestly, mystical ministry that we are being called to share with the eternal High Priest?

This is the ministry of the new covenant. Thanks be to God, we have the Holy Spirit within us, directing us, and teaching us more and more about this ministry and empowering us to lay down our lives. You know Jesus was and is priest, but He also is victim. He was priest and victim. He consecrated and was consecrated, and so to enter into this priestly ministry with Jesus the High Priest, we are also the victim. We're the victim lambs. We're the victims of our own intercession as Jesus was. Each of us carries within himself, within herself, an altar upon one's heart. The victim upon that altar is Jesus, the Lamb who was slain, residing again within us as Lamb, laying down His life as victim—a victim of God's most merciful love.

When we are consecrated by the Spirit in Baptism, He comes upon us and begins to change us, day by day, into Jesus, and so we become the victim lamb with the Lamb Himself. His ministry to take away the sin of the world has not changed. He's driven with this ministry and so He comes again to live within us to continue His priestly ministry, His Lamb of God ministry, of taking away the sin of the world.

Contemplatives get close to God, hear Him, and picking up His heartbeat, they intercede according to how God wants them to pray. There are intercessors today throughout the Church, but He needs more prayer. This is why He needs us. He needs intercessors. He needs flesh and blood. He needs bodies to come into, in order to continue and perpetuate His sacrifice on the Cross—this tremendous act of love. He wants to continue to cast fire upon the earth. He wants to continue loving His people in this sacrificial love, in this agape love, and He wants to use us now, His body here on earth, to do it.

57

God wants us to bloom wherever we are planted. Wherever God has placed us, that's where He wants us to pray. Intercession is a ministry for all people in all walks of life. God asks us to pray where we pray best—right where He has placed us. Intercession fits into any vocational call because it comes out of our Baptismal vocation, which we all have in common. That's the beauty of it. We're all in this together as a Church, as God's people. All of us together make up the Body of Christ. Together we focus on Jesus, and together we intercede for the Father's greater honor and glory.

Chapter 5

Mary, Intercessor par Excellence

When I was growing up, I always wanted to grow up and look like my mother. I didn't really resemble her too much, but when I was a teenager, one day I was shopping, and the store clerk looked at me and said, "Oh, is your mother so and so?" I said, "Yes she is. How did you know?" "Well, you look just like her." That made my day!! I was so happy to look like my mother. How much more joyful for us if we could someday resemble our Heavenly Mother!

I'm a convert so I did not always know Mary. Someone gave me a rosary at my Baptism and I didn't know what to do with it, so I put it under my pillow. It stayed there for about four months, and I began to notice so many people in Church were lighting candles in front of Our Lady's statue all the time. I thought, "They must know something I don't know." About this time, I was so madly in love with Jesus, He was enough, but now I realized my spiritual life wasn't going anywhere. I was at a plateau and I thought it must be because I needed a mother. I needed a mother to teach me about Jesus. My own mother had died when I was nineteen years old and now I was twenty-four entering the Church. I didn't know what to do, so I went and saw a priest who had a tremendous devotion to Our Lady. Every time he would get up in a pulpit and try to talk about Mary, he would cry. I thought, "I wonder what he has. I wish I had that. He has a relationship with this Woman." I went to visit him, burst into tears, and said, "Father, I don't have a mother." He said, "That's okay. I'll pray that you can meet her." And that's what happened.

It happened to be Holy Thursday, my first Holy Thursday in the Catholic Church, that I met her. I was going to spend the night in adoration at a Church called Holy Angels. I had all my spiritual books and I was going to stay awake all night. I was going to start the Holy Hour at eleven o'clock that night because that was what St. Margaret Mary use to do; I was so eager to follow the saints. Eleven o'clock came and I was going to go into the Garden with Jesus. I was going to stay awake and not fall asleep like the Apostles. I wanted to console Him all throughout the night.

I don't think five minutes had gone by when I had an image, probably one of my very first little images, and it was of Jesus. I was in the Garden with Him and all of a sudden this beautiful Lady came walking into the Garden. He introduced me to her and He said, "This is My Mother." I remember looking at her and I said, "I don't know you." She said, "That's right, but we're going to become very good friends." Then Jesus told me to leave the Garden and go with Mary. He said, "Right now, at this time, you don't belong here." So I guess He wasn't going to take me into the Agony and to the Cross my first year as a Catholic.

I had a problem with Mary when I became a Catholic because my own mother was my very best friend and the thought of a relationship with Mary made me feel disloyal to my own mother. I thought, "How could I ever call anyone 'Mother?' How could I have an authentic relationship with the Mother of God?" So the next day, Good Friday, the first thing I did when I woke up in the morning was I asked the Lord if He could possibly let me hear from my own mother. I said, "You know, the Catholic Church teaches about the Communion of Saints and I believe my mom is one of those and I really need to talk to her." And He did! Her presence was right there and I said, "Mom, I really need a mother. I'm having a problem because you're my best friend and you have always been my mother. I don't know if I can ever have any other woman in my life as my mother. What do you think? I'm talking about the Mother of God, the Mother of Jesus." The Lord in His goodness let my mother speak to me and she said, "It's all right Nadine. She's my Mother, too." From then on, I knew Mary and I would really become friends as she truly was my mother.

Believing in God's Spoken Word

Mary was praised by Elizabeth, but not only because she was the Mother of God. Elizabeth said, "Blest is she who trusted that the Lord's words to her would be fulfilled" (Lk 1:45). "Blest are you because you have believed." The faith level of Mary is absolutely awesome; we can't grasp it! She is blessed because she believed and the Holy Spirit went right along with her and the child, revealing to Elizabeth who Mary is! Elizabeth exclaims, "But who am I that the Mother of my Lord should come to me?" (Lk 1:43) How did Elizabeth know that? She knew it from the promptings of the Holy Spirit, Who probably was already prompting the prophet within her! This is a tremendous mystery of these women and a tremendous mystery of the constant working of the Holy Spirit in preparing these people for mission. This is what the Holy Spirit and Our Lady are still doing together today, with us and for us.

When we begin to receive God's Word, we need to believe it and let it take root and mature within us. We need to ponder it as Our Lady did, and we, too, will be blessed because we believed. We will be happy for "Blest are they who hear the Word of God and keep it" (Lk 11:28). God's word to us has to become part of us as intercessors. It has to become enfleshed. Believing in God's word to me literally has to become bone of my bone and flesh of my flesh. Like Mary we are called to believe that God's word spoken to us will be fulfilled.

"Let it be done to me as you say"

One time, Our Lady showed me the power of her fiat, "Let it be done to me as you say" (Lk 1:38). I was just a novice and I was having a hard time in the novitiate because bells were ringing all the time. Every time they wanted you to switch activities, they'd ring a bell. Before I was a convert, while on my summer break from college, I had a job at a large insurance company in Omaha, and it seemed like all they did was ring bells. When it was time for coffee break, they'd ring a bell. When it was lunch break, they'd ring a bell, and by noontime there were so many bells, I quit. Now I was in the cloister, still having trouble with all these bells. I thought, "Oh Lord. What am I going to do? I hate bells. It's like they whistle and a dog

comes. It's so impersonal that I hate it. I need some help here."
That's when Our Lady came.

It was the Feast of the Assumption, and she really taught me
the power of her fiat and of saying "yes." She said, "Every time
you say 'yes,' you have the same power that I had at the
Annunciation. Right now you need to say 'yes' to the bells
because behind that bell is God ringing that bell. He's calling
you to another duty, to another place, and every time you say
yes, you have the same power I had. You can bring Jesus Christ
down into a human heart right then with that kind of a yes."
Isn't that beautiful? Mary had the power to bring God to earth
through her "yes," and we also have this power to say "yes" to
God because of her. After that, every bell I heard, my response
was "yes, yes, yes!" Souls, souls, souls!

As intercessors it's important that we know our true identity.
Mary knew her identity. In her response to the angel at the
Annunciation she said, "**I am**" (this is who she is), "I am the
servant of the Lord" (Lk 1:38). How well she knew her identity
and she wants us to know our identity. We are children; we are
servants. We are totally at the Father's beck and call to allow
Him the freedom to do whatever He wills. "Let it be done to me
as you say" (Lk 1:38). I don't have to understand it totally, I
don't even have to know what the next step is, or what will come
the next day. What I do need to know is "Let it be done. I give
You freedom Lord, I give You permission. Look at Our Lady;
she gives God permission to do whatever He wants with her or
without her. When Mary gave her "yes," she gave her life.

I think Mary wants us to understand that when we give our
"yes" to God, we are giving Him our life. We are to be like
Mary, totally surrendered in the hands of God in total freedom.
Some "yeses" are more costly than others, but remember God
didn't take Mary to Calvary right away. He didn't even take
Jesus there right away. By the time they got to Calvary, with
Jesus hanging on the Cross and Mary standing at the foot of the
Cross, they were well acquainted with suffering and sorrow
through their lifetime of surrender. As intercessors, our "yes"
will draw Jesus into other's hearts and souls. You never have to
leave your kitchen! God can use us right where we are and our
"yes" will always bring Jesus.

Fiats always bring us into an unknown territory, into uncharted waters. We have not idea of the interior struggle of Mary, constantly accepting God's will and believing that God knew what He was doing! So there may be pain, but the fruit of this suffering is always joy. So like Mary, we are called to constantly give our fiat, our surrender, "Let it be done to me as you say" (Lk 1:38).

Pierced Heart

Mary had many sorrows so she was well trained and formed for Calvary. Several years ago she took me through some of her sorrows, one in particular being the real deep sorrow she felt when she couldn't deliver her baby at Nazareth. She wanted to have her baby where her family and friends were, but look where God took her to have her baby. That was hard for her.

Once I heard a priest give a meditation on Jesus' birth and how Mary must have felt when she saw the cave, the animals, and the smell of the dirty straw. She must have said to God, "Oh You've got to be kidding." God said to her, "Ride on, Mary, ride on." I don't know but she was letting me know that this was a difficult "yes" and Joseph had to give it too.

Then she was geared to come home and show Jesus off to everybody and get on with life and get settled, and then all of a sudden comes this message, "You're not going home. You're going into a foreign land." She let me see how difficult that was for her, because she was a Jew. She didn't know if she'd find a synagogue there or whether she would find any Jews there, for it was pagan country. It was very difficult for her, and she let me know, too, that after the angel first came to her and asked her to be the Mother of God, she never had any direct intervention of what God wanted. She always heard through Joseph. Isn't that amazing? The faith of this woman! but she was always able to discern that Joseph's direction was from God.

Simeon, a just and pious man, was full of the Holy Spirit, and he prophesied to Mary, "You yourself shall be pierced with a sword—so that the thoughts of many hearts may be laid bare" (Lk 2:35). Here is the piercing of the heart. There is no pain like seeing a loved one suffer when you can't do anything about it. I'm sure Mary would have given anything to have gone on the Cross herself so that her Son could have come off it. It is terrible to suffer when someone you love is agonizing and you can't do anything to help—this kind of pain comes from the piercing of one's heart by the Sword of the Spirit. It was Love, pure Love that pierced her heart.

There is so much to the mystery of Calvary and the piercing of the heart, but one of the beautiful gifts of the Sword of the Spirit is that when love pierces the heart, when the Sword of God's Spirit pierces the heart, that heart will always be open. If you have a sword in your heart, full of pain, your heart will never close—that's an intercessor's heart. Intercessors will never allow their hearts to close to anyone, anywhere, anytime. So if we allow the Sword of the Spirit to pierce our hearts, we know our hearts are open because that sword goes right through the heart. God needs that pain-filled heart for the souls to pass through for the re-birthing process again. It is a great mystery, this birthing that comes from pierced hearts.

Then Mary showed me the tremendous sorrow and pain that she went through at Cana. Remember when they didn't have any wine? She showed me that her spouse, the Holy Spirit, was prompting her to bring this to the attention of Jesus. Jesus obviously had not been prompted by the Spirit yet. So when she said, "They have no more wine" (Jn 2:3), Jesus thought right away of Calvary and replied, "My hour has not yet come" (Jn 2:4). His mind was on His Mission, but then Jesus saw, "It's her Spouse. It's the Spirit that is prompting her to ask this." So Jesus was not responding as Son to mother, but He was responding to the Holy Spirit. But the pain that Our Lady showed me was that for all these years she had Jesus to herself in the beautiful, hidden years of Nazareth. Now the apron strings were being cut by the Holy Spirit Himself and Jesus was made public. It was His first miracle, and from that point on, life would never be the same. Mary knew that His public ministry had begun and so had hers.

There's a lot of pain here at Cana, but can you see the paradox of God? Wherever there is pain, it produces joy! Like the wedding at Cana, they were going to tread the winepress and produce the wine of Pentecost, but He needs to have an intercessor willing to carry the pain, those people on mission, to bring forth the joy of the New Wine, the Holy Spirit. They always go together. Mary is so beautiful in her surrender to the very gentle promptings of her Spouse, the Spirit. Like Mary, our sufferings can help form us into a lifestyle of following and obeying the promptings of the Holy Spirit. It will always lead us to the Cross, but along with it will come the fruit of wine, joy!

Forming Us

In the Garden, we lost a lot of territory through Eve because of her "no." Eve lost that Light of the intimacy of her beautiful relationship with the Father. Eve wanted the gift of wisdom (see Gn 3:6), but she disobeyed and lost her friendship with God. Mary surrenders, says yes, and is filled with wisdom! Mary is the New Eve. She is our Mother and she is helping us to regain that territory that was lost through Eve's disobedience. Now, along with the Holy Spirit she gives this great gift of wisdom to us. The first thing Mary tells us in her public ministry is, "Do whatever He tells you" (Jn 2:5).

Mary was full of grace, full of life. We have no concept of what it means to be "full"; we have no concept of the capacity of Mary. We just get glimpses every now and then. Mary is all throughout the Bible, in the Book of Proverbs, Ecclesiastes, and especially in the Book of Wisdom, where we can read so much about Mary and the mystical dimension of her and of this light. Surrender is the highest form of Wisdom and this is why Mary is called Lady Wisdom! In the Wisdom literature, Mary is referred to as the spotless mirror of the power of God! (Ws 7:26) Isn't that amazing?! This didn't used to say a lot to me, but now in this age of the Holy Spirit, she *is* the spotless mirror of the power of God, the image of His goodness! Only God is good, and Scripture is saying she is in the image of His goodness! No wonder in her Magnificat she could say, "My being proclaims the greatness of the Lord" (Lk 1:46).

Once I had an image of this gift of Wisdom. It looked like a huge diamond, and it had different cuts and it was slowly rotating. Every time it moved, I could get a different insight into God, a different light on Truth, a new revelation of what to do or what not to do. Wisdom is a gift that lets us see what God sees, hear what God hears, and know what He knows, and He wants to share this gift with us!

It is always the Holy Spirit and Mary together who form Jesus within us. Jesus is Wisdom Incarnate. This wisdom is always being formed more and more within us. It grows within us, and it's so beautiful. The Holy Spirit needed a womb, He needed a woman, and Jesus was conceived by the Holy Spirit but born of the Virgin Mary, and this is what the Spirit does to us as well. The Word of God is constantly being conceived within us, but like Mary, we have to ponder it and digest it. We have to listen to it, respect it, and believe it, and it is especially important that we believe it.

Contemplative Prayer

"The woman herself fled into the desert, where a special place had been prepared for her by God. . .The woman was given the wings of a gigantic eagle so that she could fly off to her place in the desert, where, far from the serpent, she could be taken care of . . ." (Rv 12:6,14). This Scripture passage is referring to Mary, but also to the Church because Mary is the prototype of the Church. The eagle symbolizes contemplative prayer because eagles soar, they ride the wind. It's a beautiful, deep stage of contemplative prayer to be carried, lifted up. Contemplatives are lifted up on the wings of the eagle and they are taken to places of solitude where God can speak to our hearts. This is where we are fed, this is where we are taught. God has put water in the desert for His chosen ones to drink.

Our Lady is trying to show us that the Church must come back into the desert. The Church must come back into relationship, into the silence and solitude to hear the voice of God. That's what contemplative prayer does—we're lifted up on those wings and it's all pure gift. We're carried there, into that solitude, into that presence of God where we can hear and receive and be renewed, where our thirst for Love can be quenched, where our energies can be renewed, where we can be motivated to do what we should be doing, where we can "have life and have it to the full" (Jn 10:10). The Father is seeking those to worship Him in Spirit and truth (Jn 4:24), and this is the great gift that God gives us so that we can do that.

Mary, also a contemplative, has taught us and asked us to pray with the heart, because she's all heart. She's all love, pure love, so she is really our model for contemplative prayer. There are other kinds of prayer, but contemplative prayer is her forte, you might say. It is what she was raised in. It's what the early Church had for such a long time. Then, somehow, the Church got away from the prayer of the heart, and went more into what we might call prayer of the mind and a lot of recitation of prayers, a lot of what we call the masculine dimension. If we're talking to God all the time and that whole listening posture, that whole feminine dimension, becomes pushed to the back burner. That's why I think it's so beautiful now that Mary is everywhere with her visitations. She is calling us to prayer and she is qualifying it: prayer of the heart.

"Together they devoted themselves to constant prayer" (Acts 1:14). The Apostles and some women were together in prayer, Mary was there with them, and the Holy Spirit came upon them all. Mary was there at the beautiful gift of Pentecost. Whenever the Spirit sees her, He comes in a powerful way.

The prompting of the Spirit comes in different ways, so I want to share a few ways with you in case God is prompting you to pray a certain way, because this is powerful intercession and Mary, of course, is the intercessor par excellence. This is her ministry, because she's contemplative. It comes out of the heart, out of that knowledge of God.

Consecration to the Immaculate Heart of Mary

I personally feel that the greatest power that is lacking in intercession today is devotion to Mary. Wherever Mary is, wherever the Holy Spirit finds a soul in union with her, He comes in a special way with His gifts that lead us, direct us, and energize us because He knows our surrender to the Lord's will.

As a new convert, I read a beautiful book, *Mary in Our Life*, by Fr. William Most that said that there has to be a mystical union with Mary if you really want the full overshadowing of the Holy Spirit, because wherever the Spirit sees Mary, He comes. So for intercessors, our relationship with Mary is more than just a consecration—it's a union. Mary's heart is a burning furnace of pure love, and she is ready to give birth again to pure love (who is Jesus Christ) in souls, in hearts, in all those new wineskins, that are receptive to receiving her Son again. When Jesus is reborn again, you might say, that will be the Triumph of the Immaculate Heart of Mary. That is what Mary told the seers at Fatima, "In the end my Immaculate Heart will triumph."

We want to come into a mystical union with Mary and allow her to also live her lifestyle through our lives. We want to feel her pain, we want to feel her joy, and know the kind of power and overshadowing by the Holy Spirit that she experienced. If you want your intercession to be empowered, let Mary live in your heart, because wherever she is, the Holy Spirit is. He is her spouse. He is never separated from her, and when He sees her residing in a heart, He hovers over that heart, just like He did at the Annunciation, and that level of intercession will always produce Jesus. That's the power of intercession—when the Spirit hovers over us and consecrates us because He sees her. This is what happened at Pentecost. The Spirit came because the Mother of Jesus was there, He consecrated those gathered there, and He hovered over them. Look at the fruit of Pentecost! Nine o'clock in the morning and they were drunk with this new wine. They were intoxicated with love!

She comes as mother, but comes as the intercessor par excellence. She is the mediator of all grace, and it's beautiful to walk in the presence of Mary in this atmosphere of love. Mary wants to share all the things in her heart with us. She wants us to know many things about those Nazareth years. Mothers love to talk about their children; Mary loves to share different things about Jesus and Joseph. She loves to share her feelings and what happened when she first saw Him at Bethlehem. Mary loves to talk about Jesus and she'll share with us if we will but listen with our heart.

Mary is the Mother of the Word and she is ready to give birth again. This birthing will have Jesus coming again in deep prayer; it will actually be the body of Jesus Christ moving again.

The Church is the Body of Christ, but yet we're not fully living it at this time. People got very disappointed and upset when Our Lady mentioned to one of the visionaries that Medjugorje would be her last apparition, but after this, she won't need to come anymore. We will have the fullness of Jesus alive in each one of us! We will look at each other, and like the Apostles when they came down from the mountain of the

Transfiguration, we will see only Jesus. The Mother of Jesus will always be with her Son. She is the Mother of the Word made flesh in you and in me! God is with us! His Mother is with us! His Spirit is with us! We are the Bride and so, with the Holy Spirit, we, too, can say, "Come Lord Jesus, come!" And He is coming soon!

Act of Consecration to the Immaculate Heart of Mary

"I, N. . ., a faithless sinner—renew and ratify today in your hands, O Immaculate Mother, the vows of my Baptism; I renounce Satan, his pomps and works; and I give myself entirely to Jesus Christ, the Lamb who was slain, to carry my cross after Him all the days of my life, and to be more faithful to Him than I have ever been before.

In the presence of all the heavenly court, I choose you this day, for my Mother and Mistress. I deliver and consecrate to you, as your child, my body and soul, my goods, both interior and exterior, and even the value of all my good actions, past, present, and future; leaving to you the entire and full right of disposing of me, and all that belongs to me, without exception, according to your good pleasure, for the greater glory of God, in time and in eternity." Amen.

V. O Mary conceived without sin.
R. *Pray for us who have recourse to thee.*

Methods of Prayer

Chapter 6

"Lay Your Hands Gently Upon Us"

Using imagination in prayer

When we are in church, we are in the presence of the Blessed Sacrament, and yet we're not really in His presence if we are not aware that the Blessed Sacrament is truly there. One time I was watching the many people coming into church, genuflecting and taking their places, but very few people seemed even aware that He was there. They were going through the motions, but they were not connecting that He was really there. They were not in His presence because they were not aware of Him.

We can bring anyone into God's presence whenever we ourselves are in His presence, through our mind. For example, we can think of somebody right now who isn't in the room with us, and yet simply by thinking of them, we can bring that person into our presence. Our imagination is powerful and it can be very helpful in prayer. Jesus looks upon us as little children because that's what we are, little children, and little children have wonderful imaginations. So with our active imaginations we can bring Jesus to wherever we are, which is the whole goal of prayer.

Many people use their imaginations in their prayer through the **empty chair technique**. You can pray this way, too. Imagine Jesus sitting in a chair beside you when you go to prayer. If it will help you visualize Jesus' presence, just set a chair there, and in your imagination that will be where Jesus sits to converse with you. This can be a real way to bring an awareness of His real presence to your prayer.

There was a man who had such a habit throughout his lifetime of using the empty chair when he prayed that when he became ill and went to the hospital, he needed an empty chair by his bedside. He was so used to praying by bringing Jesus right there with him. This was his whole focus when praying—Jesus' real presence. One day he died in the hospital and his daughter found him with his head bent over the chair, resting on the back of the chair. You kind of wonder if Jesus really sat in that chair for him when he died and he rested against the breast of Jesus. That's the way he was found. Jesus said He would be with us always and He is truly faithful to His promises.

Children are wonderful intercessors. They have a beautiful childlike faith. They don't clutter things up thinking that if I pray "right," God is going to answer me. They just know that "God loves me," that God can answer their prayers if they ask because God is God and they are not. They are very much aware of that. We see wonderful prayers answered for children.

There was a family with a small baby named Julie who was very ill. The family called someone in to pray for the baby with them. Julie had a four year old brother so this man took this four year old aside and said, "Let's pretend something when we pray for Julie." Children love to pretend! "Let's pretend that Jesus is going to be here right now. Jesus is sitting in this chair right here. We're going to walk into Julie's room. We're going to pretend that Jesus is going to come into the room with us. We're going to lay our hands on Julie and Jesus is going to put His hand on top of ours. Then we're going to just see the healing Light come from Jesus' hands, through our hands right into Julie. Is that okay?" And that's what they did. He was using the active imagination as they were going through the whole scenario. We don't understand how it works, but it brings God there in a very real, tangible way. The next morning Julie was totally healed, totally. So don't be afraid to use your imagination. Don't be afraid to let that childlike gift come forth because God honors that very much.

There are many different methods we can use to achieve this deep level of communication. I'm going to mention several methods of intercession which uses our imagination. Intercession can be very relaxing and easy. It can even be without words once we make connection with God. First we always ask the Holy Spirit to come and overshadow us with His peace and presence, with His knowledge and understanding, with His gifts that we received at Confirmation.

Get comfortable, though not too comfortable(!), close your eyes and spend some time becoming aware of Jesus. Get in touch with an awareness of the presence of Jesus within you, or the presence of the Father, or the presence of the Spirit. If you have thoughts bouncing around in your mind, just let them rest. Just imagine that Jesus is flooding you with His light. Try to see in imagery the whole inside of your self being lit up by His Light. God is Light. You might imagine that you're going down to the very center of your being. You might find that it's dark, maybe it's not light. You might just let yourself sink into His presence and let His light fill you. You might find the fountain Jesus talked about, deep within you. "Whoever drinks the water I give him will never be thirsty; no, the water I give shall become a fountain within him, leaping up to provide eternal life" (Jn 4:14). It just bubbles up toward God.

Or you might imagine that you find a living flame of Love deep within. You might just imagine Jesus sitting in a chair beside you. There are many different ways you can begin to experience the peace and light; use whichever way that works best for you. You can always imagine yourself present in a story from Scripture. Imagine yourself being present at the Annunciation (Lk 1:26-38), and now you're just being over-shadowed as Mary was. You're just being filled with the living water of the flame of love, filled with light.

When you can see or feel this light, or whenever you feel yourself in God's presence, then it's time to ask the Spirit to bring to your mind one person that He would like you to pray for. When that person comes to your mind and when in your imagination you can see that person, lay your hands on the person, just as they laid their hands on Julie. As you place your hands on that person imagine Jesus placing His hands on top of yours. Imagine all the life and power from Jesus, from the Light, flowing into your hands. No words. Just let the power and the love and the life of God come through your hands to the person you're bringing to that Light. When you can see that person filled with God's love in your imagination, you might want to go on to another person. You might have a line of them at the door of your heart that God wants you to bring into His wonderful peace. Take your time over each individual. Pray wordlessly. You don't need any words. Just pray relaxed, full of God's peace. This is a refreshing, wordless type of intercession. In your imagination, see that person filled with

Light, letting the darkness go forth.

Remember to keep your heart deep in contact with the Light, with Jesus, the flame of Love, throughout your prayer. Let the fountain bubble over within you and wash you clean. Remain deeply in God's presence yourself. Let the person bask in that love that you are basking in, let them bask in that Light and Truth. If you find yourself losing contact with God's presence, return to the beginning of your prayer and return to God's presence. It's important to remain in God's presence or your intercession will not be prayer but just an exercise of remembering people. We want to actually bring them into the presence of God. Once we get in touch with God deep within us, we want to bridge the gap and get them in touch with Jesus. Always keep your own focus on the Lord.

After you've prayed for several people, you might want to rest a little bit yourself. Intercession is ministry and you also need to drink and receive yourself. You can just rest for awhile in Christ's presence, in the power of His Spirit. Then you can continue your intercession and lay hands on another person, particularly those that you love or those who are committed to your care. After you've prayed for these, you might just take another pause to drink in Christ's love, His power, His light, His presence, and His love for you. Then you might continue on and pray for your enemies, laying your hands in blessing on each one of the persons who you dislike or maybe people who dislike you or have caused you any kind of hurt, for Jesus has truly made it our obligation to pray for our enemies. He encourages us, "Love your enemies, pray for your persecutors" (Mt 5:44). "Bless those who curse you and pray for those who maltreat you" (Lk 6:28). Just feel this love power of Jesus pass through your hands into their hearts. **No words.**

You might want to pray for the nations, whatever nation comes to your mind. You might want to pray for the Church and whatever segment of the Church you feel led to pray for. It's God's power moving. He has plenty of power. He won't run out. He has enough for everybody! Don't be afraid to let your mind go blank for awhile in this restful posture and allow the Spirit to suggest persons and causes to pray for. If a person comes to your mind, lay your hands gently upon them and let God's love minister directly to that person through you.

As you go into a deeper state of union with God, God will often reveal what is in His heart that He might want you to intercede about. If you run out of people or things to pray about, you might just remember yourself now. Charity begins at home! You can end your prayer session with the words of Jesus, "Ask and you shall receive" (Jn 16:24). "For the one who asks, receives" (Mt 7:8). So it's okay to also present your own needs. Maybe you need the deeper gift of faith to really believe that God will answer your prayers, to believe that He really loves you. Maybe you need the gift of forgiveness or a deeper gift of love. Maybe you need help to succeed in something you are doing. Imagine Him giving this gift to you. Just rest, allowing yourself to be loved, to be filled with Light yourself, and listen. God may have something He wants to say. Then when you feel ready, allow yourself to surface. This is the time to journal, to write and record any of the specific details or insights you have received through prayer. Thank God for all He's done and expect it to happen.

When God first taught me this type of prayer, I tried it on a priest I felt needed to really be loved by God. He wasn't the type of priest you could go up and say, "Father, you need prayer" or "I would like to pray with you. I feel that you're empty." But God was showing me a lot of things about this particular priest and there was a lot of emptiness. This was a very intelligent man who was very heady and his heart was kind of blocked off. I did this type of prayer for him every day for about 10 minutes, no words, and he never knew I was praying. He still doesn't know it to this day and that's all I did. When I was in the presence of God, and I knew I was in the presence of God, I'd just bring him there and God would just love him—just like spiritual sunbathing! The change that took place in this priest was phenomenal! He became ignited. He came alive. It was beautiful.

This is a simple, wordless, effortless, way to pray. It's like I'm being loved and I just want to share this love with others. This is only one way to intercede, and it's restful and it's powerful. This is a contemplative way to intercede. There are many other ways. We like this method because it's a very direct contact with God and it's very effective. You can use this same method when you are in adoration, in the presence of the

Eucharist. You really don't have to tell Jesus anything. You can silently bring the people and concerns He has placed on your heart to Him, and He'll take it from there. Put them right into His love. He's there in that full Presence. It's so easy and restful. A whole hour can just fly by and you are refreshed and graces have been obtained for others. Have you ever worn yourself out in prayer? All the things we have to pray about! All the people we promised to pray for can be overwhelming, but we can hold them in our heart and connect them to God.

This is just another form of prayer. We don't have to figure out anything. It is so simple. We just allow God to touch others as He's touching us, and every time God touches a soul, things happen whether we can see it or not. God's graces and love are flowing. Every time He touches a soul, there's always something good that happens because God is good. It's so easy. It reminds me of the song by Dan Schutte, "Here I am Lord. . . I will hold Your people in my heart." That's intercession at its best. We can bring His people into our heart where God is living within us. Whatever they're doing and wherever they are, that's God's concern – He'll touch them as they need to be touched. He'll love them as they need to be loved. He knows what they need. That's why this method is so refreshing. God is praying the prayers He desires, not listening to us ramble on with directions. As long as you've made the connection and are deep in God's presence, you can pray this way all throughout the day. Just let God love you, also.

This type of intercession is just like the friends of the paralytic (Mk 2:1-12). They carried that paralyzed man into His presence, but Jesus took it from there. That was their role— simply to bring their friend into Jesus' presence. Jesus did the rest. He forgave sin, healed the paralysis in the man, both on the inside and on the outside. Like the friends of the paralytic, that's all we do. We get them to Jesus, and even then, it's not really us doing anything. It is God who brings them to our minds. We might start with people we know and all of a sudden somebody can show up from out of our past, somebody we naturally wouldn't be thinking about or praying for. The Spirit who desires His love to be poured out will help bring souls into His Love.

Our own personal relationship with the Father, Son and Holy Spirit is so important. It's essential. As God is loving you, then all you do is bring them into that Love, but if we don't know Him, we can't do this. It's like when I was a child. When I would meet somebody I really liked, I would want them to come home with me and meet my parents. I wanted my new friend to have this beautiful experience of coming into the presence of my parents. That's what we do when we love people—we want to bring them into the presence of God. We want to bring them along with us on this journey of love.

The amazing thing about this kind of prayer is that we constantly go back and forth between contemplative prayer and intercessory prayer. The contemplative prayer draws us into the presence of the Father, and then intercessory prayer takes over as we pray for whatever comes into our minds. Many people in contemplative prayer think that people or things coming to our minds during prayer are distractions, that they are being distracted from the whole purpose of their prayer and bothering this union with God, but they are not. As we come closer to the heart of God, we're picking up the burdens in His heart and the people He wants to love.

I remember when I first learned this. We were in Medjugorje for the first time. All these wonderful things were happening and I would see somebody and think, "That bald head over there, isn't that funny, but it reminds me of a man I used to work for years ago." I thought, "Hmm, distraction, get rid of it. I haven't thought of that man in years." Then pretty soon I would see somebody else, and think they reminded me of somebody I went to grade school with. This became my constant experience in Medjugorje. It was a call to intercession. These weren't distractions to my prayer, *this was to be my prayer.* God was showing me all these people and reminding me of someone else and leading me to pray a simple prayer for them, and to bring them right there with me into God's presence.

This can also be a wonderful way to pray during Mass. When these distractions start happening in our minds, we just bring them to Mass with us. Maybe something you saw on TV two weeks ago, there it is, it's being replayed right in your mind, right there in the middle of Mass. Maybe it didn't make any difference to you when you saw it, but now your heart is burning, "Oh, I never realized, Lord, they might have needed prayer." You can put them right in the chalice. It's such an easy way to pray. Using your imagination, place them right in the chalice and when the wine is consecrated, imagine them being washed, cleansed, and given new life in the blood of the Lamb. We bring these seeming "distractions" to Him, into His Divine presence, and He takes over. This can be a powerful way to intercede, which is led by God, and it can happen anytime at this deep level.

There are many ways to intercede for people. I have mentioned the "chair technique," the use of our imagination as we bring others into the healing Light of the Father, prayer before the Blessed Sacrament, and "placing people in the chalice." These are a few of the many simple ways to pray. These are gifts that have been given to us through the Church. Very simple ways to pray that won't tire us. Whenever we intercede, we must remember the Lord is the One who is in charge. All the results and the timing are up to Him. Our part is to simply be vessels through which His love can flow to touch those who need His touch.

Don't be afraid to use your imagination in prayer. Allow that childlike gift to come forth and allow God to do all the work. Throughout the day allow these "distractions" to be a springboard for intercessory prayer, allowing you to bring God's presence to others. In this way, intercessors can experience a touch of God while praying for others at any moment of their day. It becomes a lifestyle.

The next chapter will expand upon the use of images to allow the Lord to teach us how to pray.

Chapter 7

Images

When you ask the Lord to show you anything, expect Him to do just that! He often shows us here at Bellwether how He wants us to pray by using simple little images. For a long time we didn't know we could use the imagination in prayer, but we have learned that the imagination is also a gift of God. God can show us many things in simple little images because we're little children. He sees us as we are. Often the Lord has revealed His heart and mind to us through images. As many of the saints received images in prayer and in dreams, God still wants to show us how to pray today through images.

For example when five of us Intercessors were in Europe a while back, every night before we went to bed, we would always pray, "Lord, is there anything you want us to intercede for?" We would do this all the time; we would intercede constantly. We loved it! We just love to know how God wants us to pray and He does show us. We would sink into our listening posture and allow our minds and imaginations to be open to the Lord. One night an image was given of a bride without a head, a headless bride. So we asked, "Lord, what does that mean?" Nothing came so we didn't worry about it and put it on the back burner. We thought when the Lord is ready to explain it, He will. The burden is His.

The next day we were in Rome at the crypt of St. Peter. We were not dressed in habit, we were in our traveling clothes, and we were scattered throughout the crypt. I was lost in thoughts of St. Peter when this gentleman came and tapped me on the shoulder. He had a beautiful peasant-like face, pure with very piercing eyes. In broken English, he said, "Will you pray for my country?" I thought, "Now isn't that interesting? I wonder how he knows I'm an intercessor." I said, "I'll be happy to pray for your country. What is your country?" He said, "Czechoslovakia." I said, "I'll be happy to pray for Czechoslovakia. Is there any particular area you want prayer for?" He said, "Yes, that she be reunited with Rome; she is cut off from her head." There it was, our image of the headless bride from the night before! Now we understood. The Bride of Christ, Czechoslovakia, was cut off from her head and was totally suppressed. So we prayed for Czechoslovakia to be reunited with Rome, and it happened! She is reunited with her head. Through this simple image we knew how God wanted us to pray so He could move powerfully.

So whenever we receive an image, we take the picture back to God and ask, "How do You want me to pray? What is Your interpretation?" We always let God show us. This is where we need to exercise caution: we do not want to get ahead of the Lord and interpret the symbol ourselves. The Lord will show us what He means. He wants to show us what He wants to do, so the burden of interpretation lies with Him. Remember we are not operating on rational wisdom, but on supernatural wisdom from the Father. Often we won't understand how to pray with only one or two images. We need many more. This is where one part of the beauty of praying in community enters in. We need each other. As a rule, one image won't stand by itself.

We must ask the Father for the gift of faith, to renew my faith so I can continue going forward and remain teachable. We have to let go of our control and let the Lord direct. For example, during the Gulf War in 1991 there were so many ways to pray. There were so many needs that we saw and the natural tendency for us is to go into prayer and pray about all the things we thought needed to be done because we were watching it on the news, and it seemed so obvious. We each had our own particular way we thought we should pray. So we had to lay that aside and ask God, "How should we pray? How would *You* like us to pray now?" Always ask God first.

This time He said, "Pray for Israel." Through images He showed us that Israel was going to be harassed by Saddam Hussein and that Israel would retaliate. The Father showed us that He did not want that to happen. He showed us the great love He has for the Jewish people, and we also saw the great love that Our Lady has for the Jewish people. He continued to show us this in different ways until we understood what He was trying to say: He wanted us to pray for Israel not to retaliate. So every time a missile landed and they wanted to strike back, we would pray, "Please, Lord, don't let Israel retaliate" and then something would happen to help smooth things out so that Israel would not retaliate. We saw our intercession being answered and that was our whole part in the war—it was to keep Israel out of it. God had other intercessors praying other prayers; this one small piece was to be our prayer. When God reveals His heart and mind to you, and shows you something in prayer, that means He wants to do it. He's ready to move. So first of all, we seek to know His mind. We are people of the Holy Spirit and we always need to be taught how to pray by the Spirit, always.

One time I had an image of my kitty cat, Angel, and it was an awful image. Somebody was holding Angel under the water in the kitchen sink drowning her. Well I could have tried to figure out what in the world the Lord was trying to say to me, but instead I prayed, "Lord, wherever there is an angel out there that somebody is trying to kill, please stop it." While watching the news the next day, I heard that someone was trying to hold a little baby under water and kill him in a town not too far from here, but the baby had remained safe. So we don't know. We just take the images seriously and move on it. "Lord, You know what's going on. You've given me something here and You just want me to ask You to do it. You know what the image means, You know the symbol. Please do what You want to do." Sometimes we understand the image and His heart, and sometimes we don't. Sometimes we miss. There are many times we get things in prayer and we try to figure them out. We don't always understand so we don't move on it and pray the prayer, and then maybe later we hear about a plane crash and we had that information. We had it and we didn't pray the prayer.

Once I was with a group of intercessors who had the whole information on that Jonestown, Africa tragedy before it actually occurred. We didn't understand the images, so we didn't pray the prayer, and it was a tremendous lesson for me. This particular group had come together to intercede for our nation. Our nation needs prayer, and we were going to zero in on Washington, D. C. Well that sounds wonderful. I'm all for that, but this particular group had a mindset—"this" was what we were going to pray for, not "What do You want us to pray for, God?" God started giving us images about Jonestown, and we tried to think of what does this have to do with Washington,

DC? So we ended up not praying for anything. This was a high price to pay. Maybe God was going to let the Jonestown massacre happen anyway. We don't know but I have never forgotten that. As intercessors, we don't go into prayer with our own mindset. No matter how evil a situation may look or how much we know personally about that situation, we first seek the Lord's mind. On that particular day over 20 years ago, God was not leading this particular group of people to pray for the government of America; He wanted us to pray for safety in Jonestown. God was signaling us to pray for a different situation. We must always remain open to how and what the Lord wants us to pray for.

We also use images when we pray the **intercessory rosary**. The intercessory rosary can be thought of as a jigsaw puzzle made up of many different pieces, or images. When you want to put a puzzle together you usually just dump all the pieces on the table, and then proceed to turn them all over so that the colors are showing. Then you put the puzzle together, piece by piece, and by the end a picture emerges. This is similar to what we do when we pray the intercessory rosary. The puzzle pieces, or images, are supplied by God. The pieces are turned over when the Spirit is activated and we receive something—an image, Scripture, or whatever comes to mind. It can be anything. We let God put the pieces together, and by the end of the rosary a "picture" of how God would like us to pray will emerge.

We pray the intercessory rosary the way everybody prays the rosary. We follow the regular format with the Joyful, Sorrowful, and Glorious Mysteries. The difference in praying the Intercessory Rosary is that we don't decide the intentions and how to pray beforehand; rather we seek the mind of the Lord as best as we can. Sometimes we have a specific intention when we begin, such as a particular situation or person. Other times we are open to pray as the Lord leads us for His intentions. The important thing is we always begin with the concept of "Lord, teach us how to pray" (Lk 11:1).

At the end of each decade we allow for time to share what images, Scripture verses, or "senses" that those praying the rosary are getting. We share whatever we are receiving in prayer. If the images that the people praying the rosary get aren't shared, sometimes that can block the second decade progressing and other pieces from being turned over. The Holy Spirit not only gives images to us, but He also gives them to us at a specific time. He knows that perfect timing. We find that if we "hold it" or don't share what we are getting, He may not give us anything else to share. We have to release what we receive, when we receive it, and make room for another image. So if a Scripture, prompting, or inspiration comes, we share it, and it's just our little contribution, just our little piece, and the Holy Spirit then will put the "puzzle" together. If the images we're receiving are not of God, they won't go anywhere, there won't ever be another piece that will fit with it. So you don't really have to worry too much if your image is of God; if not, it will kind of die a natural death.

Praying the intercessory rosary this way is just like little children putting a puzzle together. It's a very simple way to pray. By the time the rosary is almost over, maybe by the fourth decade, the picture of what God wants us to pray about is starting to become clear. It may be a wonderful teaching, sometimes it's about our own prayer lives, sometimes it's about spirituality, sometimes it's about our nation. It may be about situations from God's point of view, like the abortion issue for example, or a situation where there is a lot of intercession needed. Maybe even a Bill in Congress. There are many things that God wants to show us; He's very interested in what we're interested in. Sometimes our prayer is about things that we aren't even familiar with. It could be about nuclear situations or conspiracies in other countries. We can "go" anywhere in the world in our prayer. Sometimes God shows us things that could happen if there isn't any intercession prayed to stop it. He's showing us a lot of prophetic things this way. Sometimes it could be a burden of the Holy Father, and through our intercessory rosary we begin to see what the Holy Father is interceding for, and sometimes God uses us to pray along with him.

It's amazing what God can be interested in! He's interested in us. His delight is to be with us, and so He loves to share His mind and His heart with us, and He will if we ask Him, if we seek it. We have about 70 Intercessor of the Lamb hermits and lay community that pray the intercessory rosary each week in this way as a community. A group of three, six, or twelve people is fine, too. Praying the rosary this way works very well in a smaller group where you can move along a little better.

Sometimes St. Michael shows up in the prayer. We believe in the Communion of Saints, and sometimes different saints show up, because they want to be part of the intercession. We have also learned so much about the hierarchy of angels, some of their missions, and what they do. We never dreamt of some of these things until we started learning through our rosary! We started to get some books on St. Thomas Aquinas to see, "Is this theologically correct?" I couldn't believe we were reading St. Thomas Aquinas! It was amazing what he wrote about the angels. His writings confirmed what we received in our rosary. God wanted to teach us about the angels.

You can certainly pray this way on your own, and we do. When people ask us to pray for a particular intention, we always ask, "Lord, show us how to pray about this situation." We don't pray a certain way about a situation just because people ask us to pray that way. We always seek the way the Lord would like us to pray. It's not always the obvious way to pray.

For example, someone might ask us to pray for their marriage, it's in trouble because of a particular reason. We will take that to the Lord and say, "Lord, show us how You want us to pray about this marriage." Or many times someone will ask us to pray that they get healed in a particular area, and many times God will honor the intercession by healing a relationship instead that the person needed healed. Or maybe the prayer will be to heal some problem with anger that this person was dealing with or something else instead of praying for the particular request of the person. We never know God's mind. Sometimes the particular prayer request is exactly what God wants to do. The person may already have that burden and God is going to honor that, but we never second guess. We always ask for it to be revealed to us, "Lord, teach us to pray." This way the prayer will always give God greater honor and glory.

So you never know where the intercessory rosary will lead you! You never know how it's going to move. It can be on the angelic world, or our world here, or it can even be for one individual person. No two rosaries will ever be the same. Many times we pray for the intentions in the heart of Mary. Once she asked us to pray for the intentions in her heart, and many times they are revealed to us by herself. Occasionally there can be an intention that Our Lady will reveal on the first decade, and then the next decade another, different intention will be disclosed. You can pray the rosary where one decade is one whole concept in itself and we pray for that, and the next decade is for another concept, but usually the entire rosary gives us one picture of how to pray.

The Lord taught us to pray the intercessory rosary with images probably for a couple of reasons. One never knows all the reasons of God, but praying this way keeps us little; there isn't any one of us that has all the answers. It's only together that we have it, and it's together that we discern God's mind. There's a protection in that togetherness. We get one little piece at a time, a little piece of the puzzle, and this helps keep us humble. We have no idea from rosary to rosary of where God wants to lead, what He wants to show us, or where He wants to direct our prayer. We simply follow.

The tendency sometimes is to see a piece of the puzzle and think, "Oh, this is blue. I bet it's part of somebody's dress." We put the piece on the table where we think it's going to go. In praying the rosary this way, we have to be careful to not put a piece in its place, or of interpreting it by ourselves. We let God put the pieces together. We let Him interpret them and show us His heart and mind so we know how to pray.

As intercessors, we don't go into prayer with our own mindset. No matter how evil a situation may look or how much we know personally about that situation, first we seek the Lord's mind. We must always remain open to how and what the Lord wants us to pray for. This way the prayer will always give God greater honor and glory!

Chapter 8

The Charism of Intercession

A charism is given to a particular man or woman throughout the ages of the Church to bring forth a very specific work that God feels is needed at a particular time in history. The charism for an intercessor, "The Office of Intercession," is to live Jesus and His Cross. Throughout our 2,000 years in the Catholic Church, we have seen many beautiful charisms given and many beautiful works come forth through these charisms. Now the Lord has seen that the charism of intercession is desperately needed.

The Office of Intercession takes place primarily at Calvary. It's the work of the Cross because it's a labor for the salvation of souls, and it's a labor of love. We are called to enter into this penitential lifestyle of Calvary love, much of which is to be lived out in our daily, ordinary exchange of human relationships. People, people, people. My godfather used to come to the cloister to visit and say, "Everything is just wonderful. I think I'm a very fortunate man. I only have one problem—people." People can be our penance! At times they are going to be a cross for us. God will put the struggle there and all we have to do is accept it. We need to struggle to accept them where they are, and love them unconditionally as God loves us. It may be costly, but we can use this kind of penance to purchase souls.

Jesus calls us to sacrifice and to do penance for the remission of sins. Jesus has asked us to enter into this kind of penitential lifestyle and it's a love lifestyle. The lifestyle of an intercessor is really living out the new commandment: "love one another as I have loved you" (Jn 15:12). Jesus loved us with that Calvary kind of love all throughout His life, but especially when He laid down His life for us. Now He is asking us to do the same for one another. He is our leader and role model. He doesn't ask us to do anything that He didn't do first. He just simply says, "Love one another as I have loved you" (Jn 15:12).

Jesus said that "penance for the remission of sins is to be preached to all the nations" (Lk 24:47). I think that's exciting! Can you imagine all the intercessors right now in all the nations throughout the world? There are so many intercessors out there and God is going to show us where they are, and He is going to show them where we are. They will hear this message of penance, they will hear the call to Calvary love, to agape love, for the remission of sin.

Jesus wants to continue taking away the sin of the world. He is the Lamb. This is who He is; this is what He does. This is love at its best—empowered, anointed love. When this kind of a penitential love lifestyle is preached to intercessors around the world and they can grasp this image and this vision, they will allow themselves to be placed on the cross with Jesus and will start co-redeeming with Our Lady again. This will bring a tremendous wave of renewal through the life of the Spirit. A tremendous force will be unleashed, a love force that no evil can stand against. There is nothing as powerful as love, but we need lovers and that is who God is looking for.

When I was with the Good Shepherd Sisters, we had many sisters throughout the world. Once word came to us from our convent in India that the teenage girls the sisters were in charge of were acting up and the sisters just couldn't handle them. It was just wild. Nothing but rebellion and disobedience running through the convent. The nuns didn't know what to do, so they started all-night vigils. They prayed an entire novena and nothing happened. They started to add a lot more fasting to their prayer and nothing happened. Then they started to make more novenas to special saints and to our Mother Foundress, and still nothing happened.

Finally the superior went into prayer and asked God, "How can this stop? This is evil and it's wearing the sisters out. We're not getting anywhere." God said, "Love can keep the enemy out. Make a novena of love." They had never heard of such a thing but they did make a novena of love. They loved each other like they had never loved each other before. They sacrificed for each other, they were sweet, they were nice, and they loved those girls as never before. They decided to love each other no matter how they felt. They lived this new commandment to the hilt! In nine days, peace came—total peace, and love, unity, and harmony were restored to that convent and to the girls. I have never forgotten that.

Love is the most powerful weapon we have. This is the Calvary love we're talking about. This is agape love. We see this kind of love power every time we celebrate Mass. Interceding for others in the presence of the Body and Blood of Jesus Himself is a powerful place to pray—we are actually in the presence of the High Priest Himself! When the priest lifts up the consecrated cup, Jesus is saying to us, "Now you do **this** in memory of Me. Do this—give your lives to Me. Surrender all to Me, lay your life down, give Me your whole life. I'm giving My whole life to you, now you do **this** in memory of Me." Here is the blood of the Lamb. This is power. He is asking that of us now—to lay down our lives as the Lamb did. This will bring such power to our intercession!

After I came out of the cloister, I really wanted to learn the wisdom of God. I was visiting founders and foundresses who were all incredibly educated. They had their calls together, they had their Rules already written, and everything seemed to just be going wonderfully for them. But here I was not knowing anything and I started getting a terrible headache about this and it stopped me. I thought, "Lord, there's something wrong here. Are You sure You've got the right person here to do this kind of work and this mission? I don't have this kind of education, knowledge, know-how, and experience like the others. I've been in the cloister all my life. I need help." He said, "What is it that you think you need the most?" I said, "I think I really need wisdom. I need Your wisdom." He said, "Fine. Read Isaiah 53."

Well, I was so excited, incredibly excited that God gave me a Scripture and I was going to get wisdom now! So I ran back to the hermitage, grabbed my Bible, and there it was: the Suffering Servant! This passage is all about the lamb being led to the slaughter who opened not his mouth. I said, "Lord, this is wisdom?" "Yes, but this is the wisdom through the power of the cross." So here we are, His little victim lambs, hopefully moving in His wisdom.

Suffering isn't the worst thing that can happen to us; wasted suffering is. There is a lot of suffering today. It can be psychological, spiritual, and physical pain. It can happen in babies, children, and the elderly. Suffering is everywhere, but so much of it is not united with Jesus' sacrifice on the cross, so the beauty and the power of allowing God to transform pain into graces for souls is lost. It's wasted pain—it's not redemptive and it's not saving souls. So we need to pray that the power and beauty of suffering gets out to the people, so suffering will not be in vain. Jesus' pain was not in vain; your loss, your suffering need not be in vain.

I was at a conference several years ago and there was a beautiful African priest speaking, and during his talk the Lord gave me a teaching about the children of Africa. "What are My children in America doing but playing games while My children in Africa are giving their lives." The blood that they are losing and the martyrdom in Africa is paying the price for what we are doing here in America. Through their sacrifice, they are obtaining the graces that we need to save our souls. There are other countries that are paying a price for the re-birthing of our Church in this country. We need to get serious about accepting and using the graces that God is blessing us with right now through the sacrifice of others. God loves us so much! Now it is our turn to lay down our lives so that others may live. Let us have our hope rekindled and "know that God makes all things work together for the good of those who have been called according to his decree" (Rom 8:28).

One of the main visions that was given on the last day of my 30-day discernment retreat for this particular charism of intercession, was the vision of Jesus Christ crucified. It was a vision of His pierced heart, and out of His pierced heart came all of this water and blood. It just flowed from His heart. What I really saw was life. He was giving birth at that time. Then the Lord showed me a huge altar with seven huge chalices on it. The life that was coming forth from the pierced heart of Jesus was flowing into the seven chalices which represented the sacramental system of the Church. I had never thought about that. When we receive the sacraments, we receive eternal life. Jesus is looking for victim intercessors to be the power behind that whole sacramental system. He still wants to continue His redemptive mission of giving life to the Church through the sacramental system and to be that Life Giver behind each sacrament. I never thought of that until He showed that to me.

He is calling us to join with Him to make up now in our bodies what is still lacking in His sufferings for the sake of His Body, the Church (Col 1:24). This is how we are going to rebuild the Church. We're going to bring it life again, and life in abundance, by allowing our own hearts to be pierced so that life can come. Paul knew this, "Continually we carry about in our bodies the dying of Jesus so that in our bodies the life of Jesus may also be revealed" (2Cor 4:10). Intercessors learn how to do this. As we hear at Mass, we learn how to proclaim the death of the Lord, which is the greatest outpouring of love the world could ever know. When Jesus held out His arms, He was saying, "I love you."

Once you have said, "I love you" to anyone, there's nothing you can say that is greater except to say it again. So this is what He wants to do—Jesus wants to say "I love you" again, but this time through each of us. He wants to tell the world again, to show the world once again that He loves them through us. "Yes, God so loved the world that he gave his only Son" (Jn 3:16), and God is continuing to give His Son now as He takes up residency within each of us. The Lord has given me a beautiful teaching on how the seven gifts of the Holy Spirit that we received at Confirmation are the tools that bring about this whole life-giving sacramental system. The way God has equipped us is phenomenal. We just haven't tapped into the many gifts and graces of the Sacraments yet.

The Apostles saw the necessity of their concentrating on prayer and the ministry of the word (Acts 6:4). That's a very anointed Scripture for intercessors. We look at the ministry of the word, as a ministry of the Word made flesh—the Word now risen in His high priestly power seated at the right hand of the Father in a far more excellent ministry. Paul tells us, "Jesus has obtained a more excellent ministry now" (Heb 8:6), that of intercession, "Since He forever lives to make intercession for them" (Heb 7:25). We are called to be devoted to prayer, contemplative prayer, that personal prayer, that intimacy and union, and of course that ministry of intercession.

This is the pierced heart of Jesus that we're talking about. The contemplative John stood there at the foot of the Cross and saw that water and blood coming forth. He saw life, he saw the Church being born, but it was through pain, through this great

Sacrifice. This is the pierced heart of Mary that we're talking about at this level of intercession: "You yourself shall be pierced with a sword—so that the thoughts of many hearts may be laid bare" (Lk 2:35). If you allow the Spirit of love to pierce your heart, know that the thoughts of other hearts are being revealed. Poison, negativity, and hatred are pouring out from other hearts in need of love.

You are in the process of redeeming with the Lamb of God Himself. Your suffering is not in vain for it's only love that can pierce our hearts. When we love someone dearly and they die, or disappoint us, or hurt us, we feel the pain, but God can use that pain that we feel for souls. He'll use anything if we allow that pain to come forth from our hearts. So we must unite our suffering with His.

Our leader today is very much the pierced heart of Mary, which is one with the pierced heart of Jesus. It's not the **hearts** of Jesus and Mary, but the **heart** of Jesus and Mary. They have but one heart: both of them have pierced hearts, they both know pain. The symbol of an intercessor's heart is the pierced heart and its beauty is that it's always open because it has the sword of the Spirit through it. The sword of Love has kept it open and it will never close. We never want our hearts to close to God or to any of His people. We are reconciling, we stand in the gap of this tremendous division caused by sin between God and man.

When I first read Teresa of Avila and the seven mansions that she talks about, understanding at that time very little of any of them except the first mansion, I remember reading that in one of the mansions Teresa went into an elevated state, which she could describe as the soul being suspended between heaven and earth. I thought, "It must be wonderful to be lifted up like that and to be elevated and just be taken up into God like that." Well it wasn't until my cloister days when I started to grow in the Spirit, that I began to realize that to be lifted up and suspended between heaven and earth is the Calvary experience. There is a power there and wisdom, but I certainly did not have any more glamorous ideas about being elevated into some mystical state!

Suffering is never wasted when we're united with Jesus on the Cross and we can help other people unite their sufferings with Jesus as well. This is where we can bridge the gap between God and man—that ministry of reconciliation where God and man are united, where there is peace and out of this union comes peace with others as well. This is the perfect fulfillment of that new commandment "love one another as I have loved you" (Jn 15:12).

Closing Thoughts:

"Truly it is Time!"

In closing, it is time to take our private prayer, our intercessory prayer, and the leading of the Holy Spirit very seriously, because it is time to regain with Jesus, the Kingdom for the Father. In fact, at this moment, there is a mighty war being waged throughout the entire world for the minds and hearts of men, women, and children. It is a warfare waged on all fronts at once, inward and outward, personal and social, individual and institutional. It is a war where the lines of demarcation are clearly drawn, not against flesh and blood, but against principalities and powers, the rulers of this world of darkness, the evil spirits in regions above. Before us is a world burdened with famine, drought, war, disease, and pestilence, with humanity rushing headlong into hopelessness and unknowingly aching for the love of God, His tender mercies, and the healing only He can give. Before us is a world whose eyes are blinded by the deception of the evil one, whose heart is filled with grief, and who does not know its God.

In this spiritual battle for souls that is set before us, the victorious Lamb is empowering men, women, and children with the Holy Spirit to collaborate with Him in releasing His life-changing power through the ministry of intercessory prayer to set the captives free. Prayer is the most strategic ministry that any Christian can have. It is the ministry most feared by Satan, and God is challenging us in this moment of history, as never before, to shake powers and principalities, seen and unseen, for His Kingdom to come. With the Holy Spirit and Mary, His Spouse, He is guiding us in a strategy of intercession and spiritual warfare, equipping the saints with weapons of love, peace, truth, integrity, prayer, and faith. Prayer warriors are being recruited everywhere to take their place in the Lamb's war.

Therefore, in this hour of darkness that faces the Church today, let us respond to this urgent call for the eternal welfare of men, women, and children. Let us lay aside apathy, materialism, mediocrity, unreservedly for Jesus, and move offensively as Spirit-led and Spirit-anointed intercessors. Let us join together to mobilize and network a massive, intensive, sustained volume of believing prayer through which God can send a mighty spiritual awakening for the world and especially to America. For, truly, it is time. I urge you to join with others in communal intercession. I urge you to be faithful to your daily time with the Lord.

Since it is out of an intimate, loving relationship with the Most Holy Trinity that our service role of intercessor flows, we pray blessings upon you now, in union with Our Lady, that the Father, Son, and Holy Spirit may descend upon each one of you as you respond to this ministry of prayer, for truly, oh so truly, it is time. We pray that with Mary, the Mother of the Lamb, all of us may be fruitful in bearing witness to her Crucified Son, to her Jesus, to her Little Lamb, and to her Risen Lamb, now dwelling in victory at the Father's right hand, so that the wealth of His glorious heritage may be distributed among the members of the Church through the immeasurable scope of His power, now alive, now activated in each one of us who believe. All glory and power and praise and adoration to Jesus Christ, the Risen Lamb upon the throne, in glory with the Father and the Spirit, forever and ever and every. Amen and Amen. May God bless you!

.

The following is an excerpt of the homily given by Archbishop Elden Francis Curtiss on May 28, 1998 at the Canonical Erection of the Intercessors of the Lamb as a Public Association of the Faithful.

"The world really doesn't understand intimacy with Jesus very well and only people who are relatively contemplative understand intimacy with Jesus. I think we see evidence of God's Providence in our lives and love for us but intimacy with Jesus is a special kind of intimacy. And so if I look for some fruits in this Family to see whether we should continue to proceed on, it's because the kind of love that Jesus was talking about in the Gospel is evident in the midst of the Intercessors and it transforms not only your lives but touches profoundly the lives of the people you touch.

Mother Nadine knows that we've been through a Canonical procedure because the Church moves very cautiously. Not everybody who says "I'm starting a new religious community" gets a hearing in the Church and only after they have made the declaration and are persistent, knocking on the door, do you get any attention. But even then you have to test the Spirit and the task of the Bishop is to discern the Spirit in the lives of a lot of people, especially those who minister in the name of the Church.

One of the things that intrigued me about the Intercessors of the Lamb is the emphasis on intercession. Somebody has to continue intercession in the world. Somebody has to constantly pray that the Church will be strong and that there will be people responding to God's grace and that out of the cacophony of sounds and sensations and pressures and powers that the call to holiness will be answered by some in our world. Because unless there are some of us who are determined to be holy, then the power and presence of Jesus is no longer perceived in our world. Somebody has to make intercession for the Church—for its priests, and I'm glad to see the priests here today, for Her deacons, and I'm glad to see the deacons here today, for seminarians, and I'm glad to see the seminarians here today, and God knows you need somebody interceding here for you to get through all the loopholes that you need to go through! You're not the only one, Mother, who has to go through loopholes! That intercession for priests and deacons and seminarians and people, people of God, prayers of intercession not just cursory, but daily and with some sacrifice, that's the kind of prayer of intercession that makes the difference. And to be willing to continue the spiritual warfare that began as soon as the first man and woman recognized they had free will and continues in our own day.

The forces arrayed against truth and holiness are formidable but yet because of the presence of Jesus and His Spirit, because we're caught up in relationship with Him that is very real and very powerful, we're willing to war, first of all with ourselves, with our own independence and passions and self-determination, so that we're willing and able to listen to God speak to us and to make known His Will to us. The greatest singular task any one of us has is to listen and to respond to the will of God. God's will for us is inexorable but we have to be willing to quiet down and listen; that's why the contemplative life is so important. Contemplative people, people of prayer, people of intercession, people who learn to listen and then speak what they hear: honestly, without fear, without hesitation.

Now the reason that I'm here to sign a document which says that the Intercessors of the Lamb are now a Public Association of the Faithful in this Archdiocese is because I have observed these processes taking place, and it seems to me that it is God's will that this work continue.

So it is a good thing that we have gathered today to receive the vows, permanent hermit vows from two of the members. Those vows are important, you know. That means you're putting your life on the line, that you're willing to commit yourself to the Lord and the mission of the Lord in this context for a lifetime. That's pretty serious stuff. And it means the community is willing to support people in vows and support people who understand something of this charism and get caught up in this charism of intercession and prayer because if there are not some who are willing to do that, then the Church flounders. We can take pride in our institutions and we can take pride in our numbers here in this Archdiocese, but what I know from personal experience and from observation is that if there are not some people serious about holiness and serious about contemplative prayer and serious about intimacy with Jesus and all that goes with that, then the Church flounders, because He's a dangerous Lover, and we find that out, all of us, and He takes us where we don't want to go and He makes us reach out to others in ways that we're not prepared to do that, and He makes our lives uncomfortable because He's so inexorable with us. But out of that experience comes incredible peace, amazing joy, and a marvelous sense that we're doing His Will. When we are able to do that then we begin to understand what it means to be lovers of the Lord.

So congratulations to this family of the Intercessors and to all of you connected with them. But with my congratulations also comes the challenge because I've learned the tricks of Jesus. The challenge is: you've just begun and you have much to do, together and individually. Jesus wants you to enter into intimacy with Him, He wants you to be lovers, and He wants you to do the Will of the Father. You've just begun! May this work which we begin today in a new and expanded way come to fulfillment through the power and presence of the Lord and His Spirit in our midst. If that happens, then we shall all rejoice at what we did today.

Amen and God bless you."

Intercessors of the Lamb

The Intercessors of the Lamb is a mixed community of Priests, Brothers, Sisters and Laity who have been called to discipleship by the Holy Spirit and formed in the Heart of Mary to continue the redemptive mission of the Lamb of God through His powerful "burden-bearing" ministry of intercession. Committed to live Jesus and His Cross for the purpose of taking away the sin of the world, equipped with tools for spiritual warfare and in the power of the Holy Spirit, we are commissioned to the powerful ministry of intercession which springs forth from the wellspring of Divine Love flowing from the pierced Heart of Jesus. In union with the Lamb who was slain, we advance and establish the Kingdom of God **within**, thus preparing the Bride for the contemplative union of Love. Our goal is to develop and foster a deep interior life in the hearts of God's people so that they might become, within themselves, "a house of prayer" (Is 56:7) as God is within Himself. Because it is the life that prays, our own personal relationship with Jesus is the root and power of all effective intercession. The stronger our union with His Heart, the more our hearts begin to beat like His…a steady, slow beat…a beat that always says, "Souls…souls…souls." Striving to cast Fire upon the earth to make all things new, we show forth the mystery of God's merciful Love to the praise and glory of His Name! Those among the people of God particularly entrusted to this Apostolate are the Shepherds of the flock to whom we commit ourselves to support through the witness of our lives and the power of prayer.

Intercessors of the Lamb
4014 North Post Road, Omaha, NE 68112-1263
Phone: 402-455-5262, Fax: 402-455-1323
E-mail: bellwether@novia.net, Web: www.bellwetheromaha.org